A HISTORY FOR THE FUTURE

STUDIES ON THE HISTORY OF QUEBEC/
ÉTUDES D'HISTOIRE DU QUÉBEC

John Dickenson and Brian Young
Series Editors/Directeurs de la collection

1 Habitants and Merchants in Seventeenth-Century Montreal
Louise Dechêne

2 Crofters and Habitants
Settler Society, Economy, and Culture in a Quebec Township, 1848–1881
J.I. Little

3 The Christie Seigneuries
Estate Management and Settlement in the Upper Richelieu Valley, 1760–1859
Françoise Noël

4 La Prairie en Nouvelle-France, 1647–1760
Louis Lavallée

5 The Politics of Codification
The Lower Canadian Civil Code of 1866
Brian Young

6 Arvida au Saguenay: Naissance d'une ville industrielle
José E. Igartua

7 State and Society in Transition
The Politics of Institutional Reform in the Eastern Townships, 1838–1852
J.I. Little

8 Vingt ans après: *Habitants et marchands*, Lectures de l'histoire des XVIIe et XVIIIe siècles canadiens *Habitants et marchands;* Twenty Years Later: Reading the History of Seventeenth- and Eighteenth-Century Canada
Edited by *Sylvie Dépatie, Catherine Desbarats, Danielle Gauvreau, Mario Lalancette, Thomas Wien*

9 Les récoltes des forêts publiques au Québec et en Ontario, 1840–1900
Guy Gaudreau

10 Carabins ou activistes? L'idéalisme et la radicalisation de la pensée étudiante à l'Université de Montréal au temps du duplessisme
Nicole Neatby

11 Families in Transition: Industry and Population in Nineteenth-Century Saint-Hyacinthe
Peter Gossage

12 The Metamorphoses of Landscape and Community in Early Quebec
Colin M. Coates

13 Amassing Power: J.B. Duke and the Saguenay River, 1897–1927
David Perera Massell

14 Making Public Pasts
The Contested Terrain of Montreal's Public Memories, 1891–1930
Alan Gordon

15 A Meeting of the People
School Boards and Protestant Communities in Quebec, 1801–1998
Roderick MacLeod and Mary Anne Poutanen

16 A History for the Future
Rewriting Memory and Identity in Quebec
Jocelyn Létourneau

A History for the Future

Rewriting Memory and Identity in Quebec

Jocelyn Létourneau

Translated by Phyllis Aronoff
and Howard Scott

McGill-Queen's University Press
Montreal & Kingston · London · Ithaca

ISBN 0-7735-2724-9 (cloth)
ISBN 0-7735-2725-7 (paper)

Legal deposit second quarter 2004
Bibliothèque nationale du Québec

Printed in Canada on acid-free paper that is 100% ancient forest free (100% post-consumer recycled), processed chlorine free.

This book was originally published in 2000 as *Passer à l'avenir: histoire, mémoire, identité dans le Québec d'aujourd'hui* by Boréal.

Translation into English was made possible by a grant from the Translation Program of the Canada Council for the Arts.

McGill-Queen's University Press acknowledges the support of the Canada Council for the Arts for our publishing program. We also acknowledge the financial support of the Government of Canada through the Book Publishing Industry Development Program (BPIDP) for our publishing activities.

National Library of Canada Cataloguing in Publication

Létourneau, Jocelyn, 1956-
A history for the future: rewriting memory and identity in Quebec/Jocelyn Létourneau; translated by Phyllis Aronoff and Howard Scott.

(Studies on the history of Quebec = Études d'histoire du Québec; 16) Translation of: Passer à l'avenir, a collection of articles originally published in Canadian, American and European journals. Includes bibliographical references and index.
ISBN 0-7735-2724-9 (bnd)
ISBN 0-7735-2725-7 (pbk)

1. Québec (Province) – History – Philosophy. 2. Group identity – Québec (Province). 3. Memory – Social aspects – Québec (Province). I. Aronoff, Phyllis II. Scott, Howard III. Title. IV. Series: Studies on the history of Quebec; 16.

FC2909.L4713 2004 971.4'001 C2004-900797-1

This book was typeset by Interscript in 10/13 Palatino.

To Jean Hamelin and Pierre Savard,
unforgettable figures on the horizon of history

Contents

Acknowledgments

Many colleagues and friends commented on the various articles that make up this book. I would like particularly to acknowledge the contributions of Jacques Beauchemin, Gilles Bourque, Jean-Marie Fecteau, Nicole Gagnon, Daniel Jacques, Bogumil Jewsiewicki, Christian Laville, Denis-Constant Martin, Henri Moniot, Pierre Nora, Joan W. Scott, and J.-Yvon Thériault. Of course, I am solely responsible for the ideas expressed.

I worked out most of the ideas that found their way into this book while I was a fellow at the Institute for Advanced Study, in Princeton, New Jersey. During a teaching leave from Université Laval in 1999–2000, I was able to revise the articles and bring them up to date with my current thinking.

I am grateful to the Presses universitaires de France, the Presses de l'Université Laval, Duke University Press, and the University of Toronto Press, as well as to the directors of the Centre de recherche Lionel-Groulx (*Cahiers d'histoire du Québec au XXe siècle)* and the editors of *Argument, Cahiers internationaux de sociologie, French Historical Studies,* and the *Canadian Historical Review* for authorizing the translation, in whole or in part, of texts originally published by them:

"Remembering (from) Where You're Going: Memory as Legacy and Inheritance" is a revised version of an article entitled "Se souvenir d'où l'on s'en va. L'histoire et la mémoire comme reconnaissance et distance," published in the American journal *French Historical Studies* 20, no. 3 (spring 2000): 277–300.

"Going from Heirs to Founders: The Great Collective Narrative of Quebecers as Revisited by Gérard Bouchard" is the revised text of an unpublished paper presented at the annual conference of the Société québécoise de science politique, Learned Societies Conference, at the University of Ottawa, in May 1999.

"What History for the Future of Canada?" is a slightly modified version of an article published in the *Canadian Historical Review* 81, no. 2 (summer 2000: 229–59, under the title "L'avenir du Canada: par rapport à quelle histoire?"

"The Fate of the Past: Risks and Challenges of Turning the Past into Narrative (Notes on Jacques Godbout's *The Fate of America*)" is a revised and slightly expanded version of an article written in collaboration with Christina Turcot and Stéphanie Vagneux and published in *Les Cahiers d'histoire du Québec au XXe siècle* no. 7 (spring 1997): 209–12.

"Toward a Revolution of Collective Memory: History and Historical Consciousness among Quebecers of French-Canadian Heritage" is a reworking of articles that appeared in *Argument* 1, no. 1 (fall 1998): 41–56, and *Cahiers internationaux de sociologie* 105 (1998): 361–81.

"What Should We Pass On? Moving into the Future" is previously unpublished.

Some minor changes and additions to the notes have been made to the original French texts for the English translation. I wish to express my gratitude to Brian Young and Aurèle Parisien for accepting my manuscript and for the excellent editorial advice they gave me in order to improve it.

Introduction

At a time when the past seems to have no future, it is said that history has become obsolete. Nothing could be further from the truth. In recent years, in Quebec and English Canada, as elsewhere in the world, there has been an increasing emphasis on finding the most accurate and appropriate way to turn the past into history. This fascination with the narrative of the past is not coincidental. In a period when all collectivities are feeling the need to renew their representations so as to meet the challenges of globalization and cultural pluralism, reexamining what has been in order to build a happy and viable future is nothing less than a necessity for those who have the power and the responsibility to make sense of the past.

In this book I focus on the debate about the future of history and memory in Quebec. This is a particularly exciting area, one in which a number of thinkers have been working to renew some of the key representations by which Quebecers portray themselves to themselves and the world. There is reason to believe that in the medium term a society that is new, at least in terms of its references of memory and history, will quietly and serenely be built on the foundations of the old one. This is what makes Quebec such a fascinating subject for study at this time.

In the following pages, readers will find a collection of recent articles originally published in Canadian, American, and European journals. Although these articles may at first glance seem unrelated, they all share a single purpose: they look at possibilities for renewal of the great historical narrative of Quebecers, agreeing or taking issue with the views of some authors who are prominent in Quebec today, and suggesting how this narrative could be amended.

What adds a certain universal dimension to this intellectual undertaking is that my central focus is not so much the past itself as the challenge of turning it into a narrative that will contribute to building a better society and establishing a legacy that is liberating for the heirs – in this case the Quebecers of tomorrow.

This approach should not be seen as in any way disparaging the scholarly enterprise. Scholarly endeavours are based on recognition of the human obligation to give meaning to the world in which we live and to which we have a supreme responsibility as custodians. This obligation to produce meaning is what sets man apart from animals and gives him an onerous moral authority over all living things. Man has the capacity to make a specific history of what the world has made of him as the all-powerful heir of creation. This capacity to recover, even redeem, the world and its past by creating a regenerative narrative is one of the ultimate expressions of man's freedom in the face of the anonymous forces of nature and history that weigh down on him. To refuse to interpret the world in a narrative that gives this world a fruitful meaning, and thus to refuse the mandate to do the work of reparation, is to consciously relinquish the human predisposition to freedom and to abandon any possibility of finally vanquishing the cruelty and banality of evil. It is to reject man's obligation to transform himself in turn into a creator and to ensure a happy future based on hope.

There is nothing opposed to scholarship in the idea that man should become a creator in order to ensure a happy future based on hope. While the quest for knowledge in the social sciences is driven by an overriding concern to reconstitute the facts as precisely as possible, it does not lead to a blind acceptance of these facts as normality. On the contrary, it is the duty of researchers to take a critical view of what they observe and record in order to create the conditions for a better future.

Of course, this does not mean, as Mona Ozouf wrote ironically, criticizing the orthodoxy of our time, that we should redress with a "well-made" history what the "badly made" past has produced – suffering bodies, warped minds, lonely hearts, miserable lives. Factuality has an uncompromising tenacity that will not allow the truth to be manipulated. On the other hand, we must resist the abdicationist view of the mind that says that the past is necessarily a closed book. Rather, it is important, as Paul Ricœur said in his masterpiece *Time and Narrative,* to give new life to the unfulfilled potentialities of the past, that is, in my terms, to be able to build the future using the "capital" of goodness accumulated by men and women of good will in the human adventure.

The obligation to reflect on historical experience from the dual perspective of vigilance and hope is what I associate with the act of thinking. Thinking requires going beyond the apparent necessity of the facts to question the meaning of human action. In this view, thinking is an act of resistance against the indifference of time and the endless flow of the contingencies of existence.

To return to the purpose of this book, thinking is – in my view – what allows man to resist the forces of the infinite past and the indefinable future by opening up, in the interval of the present moment where he stands, a breach that liberates him from heritage and expectations without breaking his solidarity with the cause of the ancestors or that of the descendants. Thinking is a way of (re)problematizing life. From this point of view, it is closely connected to an ethic of action that is not incompatible with a position of objectivity.

The conclusion of this brief argument is clear: the unavoidable and indispensable place of the intellectual is at the heart of the complex and delicate relationship between knowledge and politics, a relationship fraught with tensions. There can be no scholarly practice without a political and moral challenge that the interpreter responds to positively and that is mediated by a collective ethic of responsibility. Adopting a position of objectivity therefore consists in inscribing the narrator's quest for meaning in the narrative space marked out by rigour, hope, and dialogue.

Keeping in mind the generous and perilous goal of recounting the world and its past in a responsible way so as to build a fruitful future for the heirs, and doing so in constant dialogue with the ancestors, I intend to examine the delicate but essential question of the future of history and memory in Quebec today, a question whose implications will interest all those who reflect on the relationship between giving the past meaning, writing history, remembering, and producing common aspirations.

A HISTORY FOR THE FUTURE

CHAPTER ONE

"Remembering (from) Where You're Going": Memory as Legacy and Inheritance

In the mid-1990s, during a major discussion of Quebec's public education system,[1] many citizens asked for improvements in the teaching of history in the province. Recognizing the merits of this request, Jean Garon, then minister of education, set up a task force and gave its president, historian Jacques Lacoursière, a mandate to report on the issue and make recommendations for change.

Seven months later, the Task Force on the Teaching of History submitted its report to the minister. In keeping with its mandate, the report, entitled *Learning from the Past*,[2] presented broad reflections on (1) how history was taught in Quebec, (2) the curriculum that should be compulsory at each level of education, and (3) the objectives and content of a modified curriculum. These delicate and controversial issues, especially the last one, go to the heart of a fundamental and unavoidable question that preoccupies all societies in which the past is subject to debate – which is certainly the case in Quebec: *What* history, for what present and, especially, for what future?[3]

Not surprisingly, reactions to the report were many and varied, ranging from positive to harshly critical. To some observers, the report was an insult to the memory, history, and destiny of the Quebec people, as some recommendations – particularly those related to curriculum content – appeared to deny the centrality of the French fact in the construction of the representation of Quebec society.[4]

To others, the report – out of political correctness, conviction, wisdom, or sensitivity, or all of them combined – opened the door to a reappraisal of the narrative of Quebec's past featuring the heirs of Lord Durham on one side and those of Cartier, Montcalm, Papineau, and company on the other, eternal protagonists in an ongoing and seemingly never-ending struggle.[5]

To still others, the value of the report was more prosaic. In recommending an increase in the number of history courses at all levels of education and calling for substantial improvements in teacher training, the task force was calling for an end to the creeping marginalization of history in children's education – and the government listened![6] – thus paving the way to increased job possibilities for people with degrees in history and greater respect and enhanced social status for teachers. Finally, the report placed history at the centre of civic education, which was a boon to those concerned with broadening citizenship education through the study of history. It is easy to understand the enthusiastic welcome the report received from people who were likely to benefit from its recommendations.

It is not my intention in this chapter to reassess the recommendations of the Lacoursière committee or its appraisal of the teaching of history in Quebec. What interests me is of a different nature, probably more crucial. The problem that concerns me, and for my examination of which the *Report of the Task Force on the Teaching of History* provides an ideal pretext, is the relationship of Quebecers of French-Canadian heritage to their past, a past seen as one of ordeals and sacrifices requiring an undying memory and necessitating reparation or redemption. It is through the memory of a difficult, sometimes tragic past that the relationship of *these* Quebecers to the world, to "others," and to themselves is generally mediated.[7]

But we are living now. What is to be done with this historical despair which has been erected into a collective memory that still influences all thought about the future? How should the memory of the past be projected into the present and the future? How should we behave toward our ancestors and, especially, how should we honour their legacy while creating a viable horizon for the future? How can we build the future without forgetting the past but also without allowing ourselves to get bogged down in it?

Quebec historians and intellectuals in general have dealt little with these questions,[8] perhaps because anything related to memory and to forgetting – we will come back, at some length, to this difficult word – is extremely sensitive in this society that is constantly grappling with the inspiration, and sometimes the constraint, of its motto.[9]

Such questions should not, however, frighten those who look ahead to tomorrow. However thorny, they are unavoidable for anyone who seeks a way out of the aporias of a collective memory and history that have cast a discouraging shadow on the future. They should serve as inspiration to rise ever higher.

THE DUTY OF MEMORY

The *Report of the Task Force on the Teaching of History* was not merely a technical document for bureaucrats anxious for diagnoses and prescriptions. In some of its recommendations, it touched on the subject of the collective identity of Quebecers of French-Canadian heritage, and did so in at least two ways.

It did so, first of all, insofar as it subtly yet clearly backtracked on the necessity of dissociating history from patriotic preaching, which one might have thought – mistakenly, it seems – had been accepted since the Parent Report in the 1960s.[10] Clearly, while the study of history is decisive in the acquisition of civic consciousness and a conscious identity, it is above all, as Fernand Dumont has already stated, "a way of reminding man of his freedom to read his history and also to make it."[11] A word of warning to the patriots of *québécitude* …

The second way in which the task force addressed the question of Quebec identity was to propose that the presence of the cultural communities, the Native peoples, and the anglophone community be taken into account to a greater extent in the teaching of history, and that students be encouraged to be more open to world realities. Convinced of the need for a reorientation of the history curriculum, the task force urged the Ministry of Education to recognize in the new history curriculum that Quebec has long been a pluralistic society and to modify the great collective narrative accordingly, that is, to give the cultural communities an equitable place with respect to the role they have played in the province's history.

The authors also expressed a desire, apparently in accordance with the concerns and needs of the community, that in the core curriculum in history, including the (national) history of Quebec, the past be investigated in other ways than by applying the usual canonical frameworks of the history of Western civilization, the history of men, the history of the francophone community, political history, and so forth.

The report did not go any further, but many observers, clearly ill at ease with these positions, read between the lines and found flaws in the spirit and the letter of the document. They concluded that, in proposing to modify the accepted narrative of Quebec history, the Lacoursière committee was creating the conditions for the deconstruction and dissolution of that narrative, promoting an unacceptable revisionism, and ignoring a fundamental and founding truth of the national history of Quebec, namely, that it is a tumultuous saga dominated by the conflictual relationship between anglophones and francophones. As if the entire process of the establishment of Quebec society could be reduced to the national question.

These same observers made a second point, which was that the Lacoursière committee, in endorsing the idea of the Quebec collectivity's cultural pluralism, was relegating Quebec's francophones to a secondary role in their own history and their own society, an unacceptable and politically suicidal position, they argued, because to deny that Quebec, by virtue of its francophone majority, constitutes a full-fledged nation meant not only rejecting an objective reality but also diluting Quebec identity within the Canadian mosaic, ignoring the historical upheavals of a people, a "majority treated as a marginal minority," and the ultimate ignominy, impugning the right of a people to exist for itself and to call itself by its own name, its historical name.[12] Hence, probably, the title of a disapproving article by Josée Legault – "Histoire d'exister" (A matter of existence)[13] – which unleashed an avalanche of criticism of the report, but also some replies to those who were disappointed.

To Legault and her ilk, the phrase "histoire d'exister" had many meanings – meanings, obviously, that the Lacoursière committee failed to state or to stress enough. She therefore felt it necessary to publicly scold the authors of the report for their oversights or – it comes to the same thing in this case – their supposed refusal to address the specific situation of Quebecers of French-Canadian heritage with respect to history and memory. This specific situation was recalled bluntly by André Turmel, a professor of sociology at Université Laval, in an article – on an issue that does not interest us here – in which he harshly condemned an academic colleague, Marc Angenot, for exceeding the limits of polemic foolishness when Angenot wrote an emotional text accusing (francophone) Quebec intellectuals of a nationalist bias.[14]

Turmel's argument, which is typical of the kind of sermon that is frequently found in Quebec political discourse,[15] deserves to be quoted at length:

It seems to me that the dyed-in-the-wool intellectuals of federalism, who include you and your friends, have tackled the formidable task of giving the handful of diehard believers – business people, Anglos, the Native peoples, barons of the cultural communities, and Ottawa feds – the selling points and the logic they so sorely lack. But it is five minutes to midnight …

What separates us radically from you is memory. Better yet, the duty of memory. We remember, among other things, the expulsion of the Acadians, the 92 Resolutions of 1834, the twelve men hanged in 1838, the Act of Union of 1840, the hanging of Riel in 1885, the abolition of French-language schools in Manitoba in 1890, conscription, Asbestos, Gordon, the unilateral repatriation in 1982, Meech, and what was said to René Lévesque when electricity was nationalized: "Do you think that you people can manage Shawinigan?" We have that memory within us and we remain faithful to those men and women who wanted to build a society that would be different from triumphal Americanness. The rule of law that we have known is not the most democratic.

That is perhaps why the "Quebec democracy" that you so nastily caricature "grants" the rights of the people. A people that has not lost its memory.

In this excerpt, things are stated explicitly, and more bluntly than elsewhere. In order to exist now and in the future, Quebecers have a duty to remember their sorrows, to bear in their turn the suffering of their ancestors, an immemorial suffering branded with the stigmata of so many tragic events. As if the past for French Canadians and francophone Quebecers consisted of nothing but impediments. As if the "national story" of this community can be expressed only in terms of sorrows and grievances.

And what is more, Quebecers cannot escape this legacy of adversity and contempt except by re-founding the Quebec people as a sovereign nation, transforming the historical nature of their relationship with others. It seems there is one thing that is impossible for Quebecers to forget, and that is their having been the victims of the other. Not to acknowledge and deal with this fact that structures the narrative of the self yesterday, today, and tomorrow is to knowingly provoke in the body of the collective subject that terrible disease inherent in the political correctness and revisionism of our time, an alienating, self-negating amnesia, a refusal to recognize oneself and speak oneself as one was, as one is, and it would appear, if nothing changes, as one will be – which means a hopeless loser, a prisoner of the pathetic words "Until the next time ..."[16]

THE WEARINESS OF THE INCONSOLABLE MOURNER

Are Quebecers eternally in mourning or trying to escape from the injunction to remember – "Je me souviens" (I remember) – that defines their relationship to the world? What is to be done with this motto on all the licence plates reminding people that they must remember what they are so as not to fall into that post-modern dialectic in which, as Victor-Lévy Beaulieu reminded us ironically, "we begin to discover what we are at the moment we forget it"?[17]

Jacques Godbout has tackled this issue in his documentary film *Le Sort de l'Amérique,* which I will return to later in this book. He portrays the dilemma in which he finds himself, caught between the weighty legacy of memory from his dying father ("Don't forget, Jacques, the English burned our farms and our homes") and the puny historical memory of his children and grandchildren ("My kids and grandchildren don't give a damn about the Plains. They're playing Nintendo. They don't think about the English, the French, who fired when ..."). He is pessimistic about the future memory of his family and seems to feel completely defenceless facing the drama of memory being played out: "Yet the Plains of Abraham have become a myth ... the founding myth of Canada, since both generals [Wolfe and Montcalm] died there. There are two heroes. One doesn't dominate the other. The Anglo-French tension makes the country. If it disappears because we forgot our history what will happen?"[18]

At the end of his film, Godbout, as we might have suspected, has not found an answer; he has rejected the accepted credo. This will enrage his adversaries but will nevertheless *by default* free tomorrow's field of memory from subservience to that of yesterday.

The challenge Quebecers have to meet now is not to opt for a memory based on resignation or contempt for the past. The challenge is to distinguish what in the past should be re-acknowledged and what should be "de-acknowledged" in the name of the values and contexts of the present. As regards memory, contemporaries should keep their eyes on the future. Failing that, they remain eternally in mourning, incapable of extricating themselves from the echoes of the past, so weighed down by the past that they are soon unable to envision new solutions to the histories that they, as the custodians of a legacy of memory, have a duty to take on for posterity, eternally.

It is this obligation of custodianship and fidelity, a duty of heirs to ancestors, to the past, and perhaps to their expected destiny, that I would now like to address. I will attempt to show in what way and to what extent it is constraining. Essentially, I will tackle the question of how to remember while forgetting, and how to forget while remembering, keeping in mind that in the end the tension between old and new must be resolved in favour of the future. In order to enable the heirs to advance and to live, the past must be a springboard and a source of motivation. Above all, the memory of the past must make itself felt in a positive way, or it will become a crushing burden or source of paralyzing resentment. The role of memory, we often forget, is to enrich experience, not to delay action.

THE ART OF INHERITING

Who has not heard the universal dictum "Those who forget the past are doomed to repeat it"? It seems indisputable and full of wisdom, but has it ever occurred to anyone that its opposite might be equally true: those who remember the past are doomed to repeat it? In fact, both the rejection of the past and its total remembrance are for contemporary people, the heirs of a previous world, unsatisfactory ways of accepting and acknowledging what has been.

Rejecting the past gives rise to a destructive anonymity and creates the conditions for a drifting of the subject into an alienating nowhere. While the cosmopolitan utopia of not being anywhere, of always being elsewhere, in transit between two free zones, is the object of an intoxicating quest by the new "globalists," it must be acknowledged that, for the vast majority of people, the idea of being a "citizen of the world" or the "ultimate mutant of human evolution," that is, of having a limitless sense of territorial and historical belonging, is impossible and even frightening. To interact with significant others remains a heartening prospect for many people afraid to confront the anxieties of the inner quest, the confusion of the universe, and the uncertainty of the future without references or paths.

For most people, unlimited space and infinite time are anonymous references, evoking absence and solitude, a desert, rather than presence and completeness, a justification for existing and a possibility of being. For them, remembering the past – or, what amounts to the same thing, feeling a connection or relationship to a continuity, a historical and territorial place that is *situated* and *inhabited* – offers freedom from insignificance and banality. It gives them the impression of having been chosen, that is, of having emerged from indifference and obscurity. If remembering the past is for the subject a source of completeness with others, a process of integration of the self, and a way of finding meaning, the rejection of the past is actually impracticable since it leads to the reduction and impoverishment of the person, which is a tragedy.

As has been said time and time again, you have to be a citizen of somewhere for travel to have meaning, you have to possess a homeland to put otherness into perspective. The moral is clear: you must be conscious of where you come from in order to avoid disappearing in the reel of human destiny, to escape self-negation and desolation. "Freedom needs a world," as Alain Finkielkraut said in a recent book.[19]

This said, it would be wrong to think that remembering the past is only liberating. On the contrary, when it leads to the ancestors' domination of the world of the living, it can obscure the self.

What is to be done, then, with a motto as powerfully suggestive as the one that marks Quebec identity: "Je me souviens"? Accept it as a solemn command of the forefathers, or get rid of it as a burdensome inheritance? What is the nature of the connection that should be established with ancestors in order both to respect their memory and to win a very personal place in the evolution of things? How can heirs shape their sense of history and situate themselves in relation to a specific continuity of memory without jeopardizing the possibility of exploring new territories of identity?

There are no simple answers to these universal and eternal questions. There are, however, a few propositions that seem to me reasonable and helpful in organizing the present while dealing with the apparent dissonance between the forces of the past and those of the future. I say "dealing with," because the process of reflection that leads to the organization sought, that ultimately provides the form and the substance of the historical consciousness of living, thinking subjects, requires in the end that a choice be made. It is not possible to both embrace and reject the past; one has to go beyond the aporia by framing the problem differently. The following proposition is interesting from this point of view: "To honour one's ancestors is to be accountable to the future."

The appeal of this proposition is clear. For the heirs, there is no question of shutting themselves up in the universe of the unforgettable evoked in the injunction to remember, which takes over the future and obliterates it. The burden of memory on the lives of the descendants and on their horizon of expectation would be an insurmountable constraint on their present and immediate future. It is impossible from any point of view to envisage a legacy with such an annihilating effect on the future. The heirs have their lives before them. If they want to be the responsible custodians of a heritage for which they are indebted to their ancestors, a heritage that contributes objectively,[20] if not positively, to defining their identity, the fact remains that their historical mission – if it is still possible to use this language of transcendence which is rejected these days – is to renew the community so as to find their way and their meaning. Without this effort of renewal, the future is condemned to being nothing but an eternal return, as if caught in the trap of a founding imperative. To live, it is necessary to free oneself from the past, which does not mean repudiating what has been or despising the recognition ancestors are due. But it is important to be critical of tradition and hence of one's heritage, which is never carved in stone.

By "be critical," I mean, in sympathy with the descendants' cause and in order to build an open future, to reflectively distance oneself from the constraints knowingly or unintentionally created by ancestors. As Fernand Dumont aptly wrote, although in the context of a different argument: "We may see the traces of the past as testimony with which we feel solidarity without necessarily identifying fully with it, testimony which we in turn will provide; if we reject these traces, it is not because they did not exist but because they contradict the values we have chosen for the conduct of our lives."[21] In other words, the commitment to tradition and continuity, so that everything is not just the ephemeral moment, depends first of all on the search for meaning, the goals, and the refusals of the living. In a reversal of memory in favour of the future, it is the ancestors who must show solidarity with the goals of contemporary people, and not the opposite.

This idea of solidarity in favour of the descendants needs to be clarified. In my mind, solidarity here implies the mutual responsibility of ancestors and heirs, based on a kind of intergenerational friendship, hospitality, and generosity. Far be it from me to say that descendants have total licence and may if they please get rid of some previous presence, making a kind of tabula rasa of the past; that would be throwing out the baby with the bathwater. In practice, heirs have the extremely heavy responsibility of making their legacy bear fruit, that is, of capitalizing on their ancestors' contribution in order to increase the accumulated benefits of goodness. I am talking here about goodness in the sense of what is enriching, what is favourable to human development, what opens up the horizon rather than closes it, what is admirable and illuminates the darkness. Every generation produces its share of goodness and harm. The responsibility of heirs is precisely to exploit the capital of goodness accumulated by the ancestors, to make it the point of departure for their own specific quest, and to strive in their turn to increase it for the benefit of their descendants. In the operation of converting the accumulated capital into new capital of goodness – an operation that is based on a process of critical reflection and that leads necessarily to difficult questions of collective ethics – there are losses and gains of meaning.

While it is clear that meaning is at least in part passed on from generation to generation – that is, that the heritage of the past objectively marks the present even when it is not subjectively adopted by the descendants – this meaning is nevertheless itself transformed to meet new needs, unforeseeable by the ancestors, that arise in building the present. This transformation is crucial. It is the essence of intergenerational transmission, the ultimate purpose of which is the advancement of humanity. Clearly, while heirs can be very close to their forebears and draw on their values and actions, their questions and decisions are nevertheless determined by the realities of the present, insofar as they can grasp its complexity while trying not to obscure the future (too much). Hence the idea that love for ancestors should be the heirs' consciousness in relation to what is to come.

The responsibility of ancestors is dual. They must, of course, produce goodness rather than harm – a difficult challenge, given the uncertainties and complexities of real life. They must also be able to "die," that is, to refrain from ending the history in which they themselves are actors. Ancestors are obliged to leave the heirs to engage with their own destiny.[22] They must envisage their death as a moment of redemption or liberation. This is what we are taught by certain dogmas whose wisdom we have misused. Death is redemption and liberation because it allows the future to actually take place without being mortgaged by the past. In a sense, death is a gift of the self for the benefit of posterity, justice before life and for the benefit of life. Death can mean, depending on the situation, the end of suffering and the release of the survivors from the sorrows of the past, or the sowing of the seeds of the future with the goodness achieved during one's lifetime. Unless it is liberating, death is meaningless and inconsequential – as life may have been before it – or, what is much more serious, it usurps the future.

And herein lies, in part, the tragedy of Quebecers of French-Canadian heritage as a community of memory and history. Inspired by their great intellectuals – the melancholy scholars and poets of an apparently failed or constantly postponed refounding of their people[23] –they tend to remember the mistakes they have made, the pain caused them, what they did not do, or what they could have done, rather than emphasize what they did or are doing that is right and good.[24] In practice, these Quebecers carry their past like a cross. For them, despite what many historians are now telling them loud and clear,[25] the past is a breeding ground of painful, depressing memories rather than a pretext for positive remembering. Worse still, Quebecers of French-Canadian heritage maintain this obsession by perceiving their progress as a prelude to disaster rather than a sign of success.[26] Stuck in an inconsolable sadness resulting from their supposed situation as "failed rebels,"[27] they are unable, or barely able, to escape from the imaginary of a victim and the mentality of a person owed a debt. To grow up, they have been told and are still being told, you have to suffer. Between their "old" identity as French

Canadians and their supposed new identity as Quebecers shaped by this heritage, there are as many continuities as ruptures, if not more. That is why the past, rather than being a source of motivation and hope, remains for most of them a place of intolerable alienation that requires reparation.

The past, the product of the action of ancestors, is a capital that contemporaries must place themselves in a position to exploit, a heritage they must use as a base from which to go forward to colonize the future. As Fernand Dumont also said, "It is important to discern what in the past deserves to be re-acknowledged [and, I would add, what deserves to be 'de-acknowledged'] in the name of the values of the present."[28] Otherwise, memory becomes nostalgia or resentment, or, worse, it gives rise to impediments.

The terms *re-acknowledged* and *de-acknowledged* are important here because they imply that memory (the past re-acknowledged) is the active, conscious, and therefore selective, remembering of what has been in order to extend its positive impact and favour the primacy of good (or good effects) over bad (harmful effects) in building the future. In the case of forgetting (the past de-acknowledged), the liberating amnesia consists less in ignoring, repudiating, or erasing what has been than in deactivating the bad (or the seeds of harm) so as to grant amnesty to what has been, liberate oneself from one's enduring furies, and free the future from what could prevent it from blossoming in a "renewal."

It cannot be overemphasized that choice in relation to memory is unavoidably a matter of collective morality and political culture and is carried out in keeping with the stakes and challenges of the present. This process of choice is also known as the work of mourning, which comprises selection, internalization, reappropriation, and updating of the past. It is the transformation of the past into a heritage of hope. Through the transformation of the past into memory, the work of mourning ensures the survival of positive values projected into the future. In practice, mourning is nothing less than an act of re-foundation and regeneration that makes it possible to move on to other things. The work of mourning is neither discharge nor renunciation, but rather the production of meaning, in favour of life and the future.

It should be understood that the motivation for choice in relation to memory is not to reduce the past to silence, but to draw from it a capital on which to build the future, honestly taking into account the situation of the contemporaries. Without the quest for positive values, the present remains inexorably in the shadow of a past that exudes sombre memories. There are memories that leave the heirs powerless, that, like vampires, suck the life out of the future, memories that kill contemporaries' passion and ambition. The past should never be allowed to limit or extinguish the future for the descendants. One does not redesign a house to accommodate an inherited object. Rather, the object, placed in its new context, is reinvested with a meaning that will perpetuate the presence of yesterday in the creation of tomorrow. The same is true when one inherits an entire house: if that house is not renovated, it quickly becomes a coffin for its inhabitants. Unless there is a renewal, time causes the structure to disintegrate, beginning a cumulative process of deterioration. Renovation is not a betrayal of the past; it is an updating of the old in keeping with the challenges and constraints of the present. It is what allows the old to endure. The stakes of today should determine the uses of the old. Unless it is reclaimed for the present, the old dies forever, which is deplorable. With no past, the present risks falling into "absense." But if the past outweighs the present, it can lead to a vicious circle of repetition. As great thinkers have repeated ad nauseam, there is an art of inheriting that consists in updating what is transmitted, conserving it while modifying it. It is on this condition alone that heritage contributes to freedom.[29]

Hence the proposition that history and memory must be both recognition and distance. I mean that the relationship of heirs to the(ir) past can only be one of relative emancipation. Without this salutary emancipation, which is a duty as important as that of respect for ancestors, the descendants remain prisoners of an unforgettable heritage that weighs on their destiny like a mantle of lead. While the heirs are decisively marked by the actions of ancestors, history cannot take the place of being for them. In practice, moreover, societies develop through the heirs' insatiable (re)conquest of the past. It is through this liberation from the past as a result of critical reflection by the heirs on the actions of their ancestors that society creates the conditions for transcending itself and advancing through future human action, and that it is able to give rise to new events that mark its evolution in time. In and through the actions of the heirs, society emancipates itself from a memory that would otherwise crush it.

The perspective of "Je me souviens," as it is often exploited in public debate in Quebec by those anxious to remind supposed amnesiacs of their "duty of memory," offers heirs a disheartening option for the future, an option as senseless as the pure and simple forgetting expressed in "Je m'en vais" (I'm leaving), which a young, politically depressed (former) Quebecer, Hélène Jutras, proclaimed in the public arena, provoking strong reactions in the community.[30]

The positions taken by Legault and Turmel, described above, were indeed discouraging, not in relation to some other position that would be objectively more correct – the assessment of the opposing arguments is not what interests me here – but because they involve the total reification of the idea of the *unforgettable* as the matrix of collective meaning, the legacy to be transmitted, and the horizon toward which to project oneself. This same dependency, this same subjugation to an undying past is evident in the following words by Serge Cantin: "Ultimately, I would say that in Quebec one does not choose to be a nationalist: one is a nationalist by necessity, the necessity dictated by the future of one's self in a nation to which one knows one belongs and to which one acknowledges a debt, a nation one would have to be blind or in bad faith to claim is not threatened. Hence we are nationalists too, let us not be afraid of the word, out of duty: the duty the dead impose on the living to 'reappropriate something of what they have felt in order to make somewhat intelligible what they have experienced,' in Fernand Dumont's marvellous words."[31]

Such a perspective is clearly unacceptable for the descendants, who have an obligation to keep the possibility of choice open – the fundamental choice that I spoke of above and that I consider to be the very expression of the historical consciousness of the thinking subject – and to struggle to maintain control of it. It is by "remembering (from) where they are going" that the heirs can best reconcile the past and future dimensions of their present.

Despite the apparent ambiguity of this expression, it implies a clear position with respect to identity: the past cannot be that place we inhabit eternally, where we conceive the future and take refuge from the assault of the complexity and uncertainty of the present. On the contrary, the past must constantly be redeemed through action and questioning in the present so as to build an open future.

"Remembering (from) where you're going" means precisely undertaking this operation of questioning and redemption. It means taking on the work of mourning as one who grieves, not as one who is aggrieved. It means no longer stirring up the sediment of losses and instead transforming the consciousness of those losses into a source of creativity. "Remembering (from) where you're going" means finding ways to think about the past while binding its wounds; it means seeking in the past the impetus to go beyond the old torments rather than constantly coming back to them. "Remembering (from) where you're going" means re-articulating the historicity of subjects and communities around a structuring principle of collective action, the principle of memory as recognition and distance. It is in the tension between recognition and distance that the heirs' place of memory – and of identity as well – is to be found, with and against their ancestors, a place of memory that testifies to the place of man himself in the duality of his consciousness, irremediably divided between the past whose continuity he ensures and the horizon that calls to him indefinitely, between a presence that cannot fulfill him and an absence he strives inescapably to fill.[32]

THE HISTORIAN AS EDUCATOR AND RELAY RUNNER

It is possible, even necessary, to disobey the appeals and summonses of the past. What is more, historical consciousness is the inevitable product of a choice by contemporaries. And it is perhaps the fundamental vocation of the historian – in addition to illuminating the extraordinarily complex material of the past through scholarly work – to stimulate, harmonize, and enrich with rigour, subtlety, and hope the process of reflection that leads to this (re-)founding choice that has the potential to be emancipating and redeeming.[33] At least, that is what I am proposing.

The historian's main mandate, it is widely felt, is to prevent man from drifting senselessly, by reminding him of his origins. This reminder is needed so that he may avoid being absorbed in and by the uncertainty of the future. Without this saving reminder, man is considered powerless. He not only lacks the impetus to move forward, but becomes the unfortunate victim of oblivion, the Minotaur of lost souls. Without full historical consciousness, man is recognized to be unconscious. He drowns in the waters of the Lethe. He develops in a state of amnesia, which leads inevitably to uncertainty and the loss of the capacity for reflection. As a result, he can only repeat his blunders, following the siren songs of the ephemeral and getting drunk on senseless exiles.

Without historical consciousness, people are no better than lobotomized animals. Fernand Dumont said as much in his classic article on the social function of history, published in 1969; he was fundamentally concerned by the ravages resulting from the hold of technocratic ideology over collective historical references and social ties. Most of the authors of briefs to the Estates General on Education or the Task Force on the

Teaching of History, sharing the same concern and using a fashionable cliché, also spoke of the need for the study of history in order to fight the spectre of irreparable forgetting and to regenerate consciousness – patriotic or civic, depending on the individual – particularly in young people.

But what if the study of history, instead of encouraging people to remember the past without any obligation to think about their heritage, gave them the means to rise above the past by playing dialectically, in a constructive way, with what is unsaid and what is remembered?[34]

There are times when the surplus of memory finally makes one believe in the end of things, drying up hope instead of generating it, and weakening the individual and collective capacity to project oneself into the future. To some extent, this is the situation now in Quebec. It is wrong to think that people in general, and young people in particular – I am talking here about Quebecers of French-Canadian heritage – are ignorant of their history. On the contrary, they know it quite well, in the sense that they have grasped the central principle and the main framework of *one* narrative of Quebec and Quebecers, namely the one of a people with a tragic destiny, a people that was for a long time backward, oppressed by the clergy and by the English, and that has succeeded in part in averting the terrible fate looming over it by re-founding itself through the Quiet Revolution, a great collective move forward.

It is quite possible, I readily admit, that a large majority of people, perhaps more young people than their elders – but this remains to be seen – know nothing more than this of their collective history, especially if they are asked specific questions, for example, to place events or individuals in context or locate them on a timeline. There are abundant examples of anachronisms and basic mistakes, some funny, some discouraging.[35] But this is not a fundamental problem of collective amnesia due to absence of historical knowledge. The "absence of memory" diagnosed by many experts wanting to hear precise answers to factual questions is quite simply a result of false expectations concerning the historical knowledge the general public is likely to assimilate. People obviously know what the (francophone) Quebec collectivity considers to be the heritage of memory that should be passed on to current and future generations.

While it is difficult to know to what extent people actually identify with this memory and draw on it practically or politically, it must nonetheless be acknowledged that its substance is widely accepted. This may be seen in the following quotes from essays by undergraduate students in history who were given the following task: "Describe the history of Quebec from the mid-19th century to the present as you know or remember it. You may structure your text as you wish, emphasizing the elements you consider important, regardless of how the history of Quebec is generally presented."[36]

- To me, the history of Quebec is a succession of struggles for recognition as a society. The history of Quebec is a beautiful saga that takes place over almost three centuries.

  However, since the mid-19th century, the only important fact, in my view, is the importance of wars. Even though they are representative of society throughout the world and the perpetual struggle between "good guys and bad guys," you also have to see in them the struggle of Francos and Anglos that has being going on forever.
- I see the history of Quebec as a constant rivalry between anglophones and francophones … I would like to emphasize the fact that the history of Quebec as I see it is one of anglophone dominance over the Québécois, both economically and politically. Of respect for the Americans, in World War I, by the Québécois, who were simple farmers and were led by the Catholic Church. In short, the Québécois have always been dominated by another people and have been hesitant to take charge of their own country.
- I have very few actual memories with regard to the history of Quebec, obviously. The perception I have always had – and that I still have a little, in spite of information from courses on the his-

tory of Canada – is one of a people that was backward, rather uneducated, dominated by fear of the all-powerful clergy, and that managed to stay more or less stable until 1960.

- I see the Quiet Revolution as our awakening – the "springtime" of our people (much more than 1837–1838) – which brought Quebec into the world. I know that this is a little bit inaccurate, that changes take place over time and that they began well before 1960, but I have always had the perception that 1960–1966 was a crucial time. After that, the development continued at a varying rate, depending on the conditions …

  Finally, I have always – perhaps this is because of my teachers – seen Canada as an endless war between French and English.
- The history of Quebec has always focused more on political than social history. It is the history of the struggle of francophones for survival in an anglophone world. The entire social history revolves around that. It is a struggle against assimilation, a struggle for provincial autonomy. Economically, Quebec has been somewhat behind Ontario. An economy in which agriculture is very important.
- Urbanization took place gradually in Quebec. The Québécois were poor. Many Québécois went into exile in the United States. The economy was controlled by the anglophones. Gradually, the Québécois have asserted themselves and have got rid of their complexes. With the Quiet Revolution, the Québécois opened up to the world and Quebec society modernized and got in step with the rest of the world.
- The history of Quebec is in my opinion based on domination by the British or the English here. It is the history of English-French competition based on trade and profits … To me, the history of Quebec is only about wood, fish, or furs. It is a people that has never been able to stand up and make its demands loud and clear. I would not go so far as to say that we are not fated for success, but our ambitions sometimes seem to make us feel that. We have not done anything major to distinguish ourselves. The history of Quebec does not really have any story to tell, we are too young a people. One day, perhaps, other generations will have something to learn about besides Indians, wood, fish, and furs.

- My perception of Quebec has for a long time been based on courses I have taken as well as common-sense information. The Quebec francophone was marked by various aspects of life. Religion appears very important to me, it marked the daily lives of rural people, their way of thinking (their submission to the Church and to Anglo-Saxon interests). The rural nature of francophones also prevented them for a long time from having an industrial mentality, it was only after the [Second] World War and with the Quiet Revolution that their values quickly changed.

In these excerpts, of which I could have included an infinite number, the students demonstrate not the slightest uncertainty, but rather considerable assurance concerning their knowledge. I will try to identify the key ideas:

- Young Quebecers of French-Canadian heritage know that the destiny community they belong to, whose heritage they, "tomorrow's ancestors," must carry on – as was hinted to them in a famous document[37] – has been difficult. Their fate was decided long ago: they are part of the procession of the oppressed. They are the descendants of a lineage that has had to face terrible calamities in 1759, 1763, 1774, 1837–38, 1840, 1867, 1917, 1942, 1982, 1990, 2001 – with more to come.[38]
- These students also know that the people whose dependents and trustees they are was for a long time in the grip of a kind of "evil beast," the "two-headed other," the first head of which was "the other within" – the clergy, Duplessis, traditionalists, federalists, etc. – and the second, "the other outside" – the English, foreign capital, the federal government, sometimes Americans, etc. Fortunately, thanks to the period known as the Quiet Revolution, this people has succeeded, at least in part, in emancipating itself, modernizing, and thinking it might find a way to exist without being under trusteeship to others.
- These young people know, finally, that the culmination of the great Quebec journey in history will be when the will to

> exist without being under trusteeship leads to a decision by the community to free itself from the grip of the "two-headed other."

What more can we ask? It seems that (young) Quebecers of French-Canadian heritage actually identify with what some, who take pride in this, would probably call their "tabarnaco" history, a kind of modern, decolonized version of the ideology of *la survivance*.[39] This is the narrative that primarily fuels their collective identity.[40] In fact, their memory is precise in that it is simple, focused, and assured. And that is certainly a problem, if not a failure, in terms of a memory for the future.

Contrary to the claims of the preachers worried about the survival of the French fact in Quebec, there is no lack of memory, but rather an excess of memory – or, at least, the abuse of *a* memory. This situation hampers discussion of the idea of some new beginning, with or without (English) Canada, in continuity with or against "our" past. What the (francophone) Quebec collectivity – like the (English) Canadian collectivity, for that matter – needs at the present time is air to ventilate, broaden, or defocus its accepted memory.[41]

While it is true that memory – more than just time, which has no moral meaning or purpose – heals wounds, perhaps we will have to learn also to forget, that is, to think of history in terms of mourning and possibly healing the wounds it leaves. There is nothing far-fetched about this idea. According to traditional wisdom, forgetting, far from the negation of remembering, is the most perfect form of remembering, and its ultimate transcendence.[42] An interesting paradox. But what is meant here by forgetting still has to be defined.

In my understanding, forgetting does not have any negative connotation, nor does it constitute a refusal. Forgetting is not a way of repressing or annihilating the past or of silencing the memory that could be born from it. It is, rather, the culmination of mourning, which, turned into forgiveness, opens a universe of the future, of possibility and understanding, based on the recollection of the good in the past rather than the harm. In this sense, forgetting is a transition, a transformation. Similarly, the concepts of mourning and forgiveness do not here mean abandonment, loss, omission, amputation, renunciation, abdication, or anything like that, but rather a predisposition to a regenerative new beginning. This desire for a new beginning is justified in a way that seems legitimate to me – the past cannot be changed, so why get bogged down in it?

What is at stake – and this is the challenge for the heirs – is precisely to go beyond the condition of their ancestors. The past cannot be set up as master, or it becomes hell. Nor, as Emmanuel Lévinas says, does it allow us to focus the present moment through images from memory, or the future through foretastes or promises. Like forgiveness or indulgence, probably, the past is useful only to enable contemporaries to lift themselves up. The fact that the past has been painful and that it still bears the marks of accumulated injuries does not change the moral obligation to distance oneself from it so that the wounds can heal. In some cases, this distancing process also demands that the lesion not be sutured but that its potential for scarring or catharsis be explored. As Sören Kierkegaard said, we should not be afraid to leave the wounds of possibility open in order to regenerate bruised bodies. To which I might add that hope should be at the beginning of history and of the memory of the past.

In this delicate, complex, subtle – even, because of the uncertainty involved, dramatic – transformation, through mourning, of wounds into possibility and of memory into regenerative consciousness, historians are called on to play an irreplaceable role as brokers, bringing together their qualities as scholars and their responsibilities as citizens in the enterprise of regeneration. For this reason, I see the historian as an educator and a "relay runner," someone who in keeping with rules and procedures, professional ethics, critical judgment, and faith in the future takes part in the process of transmission.

Historians, as those most qualified to ensure the past's effective fulfillment in the present with ethical and scholarly rigour, are also the ones who can best reconcile the apparent contradiction that exists between the loss and the gain of meaning in the evolution of things and the succession of generations. In my view, historians are not really the guardians of the past, the vestal virgins of time. They are the ones who transmit memory, who, based on the irreducible, teeming factuality of the past, present the panoply of possible paths to the future. Historians are the ones whose role is to "pass on the past" in a history that is not only the result of critical reflection by contemporaries, with and against the ancestors, but also a herald of the future and of hope.

What should at all times guide historians in their quest for meaning in the present-past is respect for the extraordinary complexity of the facts and the need to create the conditions for an open, better future. Their role inevitably takes them to the heart of problems of collective morality: as scholars and initiators of democratic debate, they have to work in favour of the good over the bad, by which I mean in favour of hope over pain, and of deliverance over animosity.

Through their work of writing the past as history, historians must strive to open the future as wide as possible. They have to create conditions such that the concept of fixity never prevails. They must remind contemporaries that the past only in part determines the horizon of their choices and that those choices constitute their freedom to make their history both in continuity with and against their ancestors. The ultimate role of historians, which gives fundamental meaning to their scholarly and civic activity, is to constantly encourage the men and women of their time to ask themselves not what they must remember in order to be, but what it means, in light of the experience of the past, to be what they are now.

It should be noted that these two questions entail very different responsibilities for heirs as subjects. The first question ("What must I remember in order to be now?") attaches them to a memory on which they must remain dependent, perhaps without wanting to, so that in order to exist socially as beings within a continuity of time, they must fulfill the duty of memory. Their mandate is clear: it is to nurture their ancestors, who, in a peculiar reversal of perspective, become their descendants. The second question ("Who am I by virtue of my past?") leads heirs as subjects, as participants in present and future collective life, to place their lives in the context of a movement in which they have a stake and which they are urged to build in the present, together with others, drawing more or less on the actions of their predecessors. In this perspective, they are or are not nurtured by their ancestors, who take their places once again – quite rightly, I would say – as forebears.

It should be understood that being a link in a chain does not mean being chained to the succession of previous determinations, but rather playing one's part in the ongoing enterprise, made up of gains and losses, additions and deletions, of building the world. Similarly, in this scenario the past does not appear as the pretext for an irrefutable, compact, exclusive demonstration of the events leading to the present – the present enlisted to serve the logic and the burdens of what has gone before. Rather, the past reveals itself as an unlimited universe of values created and tested by the ancestors, a universe in which contemporaries can draw inspiration, though not lessons or recipes, to soothe the unbearable anxiety arising from their lightness of being.

It is in these common values, a sort of transcendental "precipitate" of human action in time, that people of today can, as historical actors responsible for the evolution of their world – one can always make a liberating history of what the world has made of us – discover the common aspirations that motivate them to raise themselves ever higher.

FOR A HISTORY OF THE FUTURE

History is the work of producing meaning that is indissociable from an ethical reflection on remembering. The role of historians is to remind heirs that they have a duty to "remember (from) where they are going," and that the only demand that comes to them from the past is the obligation of mediation in the future.

Through the narratives they create, the inventive resources of which surmount all obstacles and justify all hopes, historians are situated at the centre of a paradoxical convergence that is essential to the continuity of the world – and that, according to Hegel, is the very engine of historicity – between the impossibility and the inevitability of forgetting and forgiveness. Such is the responsibility that falls to them.

There is an infinite dialogue – but not a relationship of causality, much less teleology – between past, present, and future. I would suggest that the heirs know this, without always exercising their right to freedom. Very often, it is their predecessors who, associating their time on earth with a certain finitude of history, mistakenly believe they hold the key to the fate of the heirs.

If there is, as it is said, a crisis in the transmission of history, it perhaps has less to do with the refusal of heirs to situate themselves in relation to a certain continuity and a certain tradition than with their hesitation to acknowledge an unsatisfactory heritage of memory that is incompatible with their political imaginary. In this perspective, the problem of the heirs is not to ensure the continuity of the past, but rather to understand the history of the forebears and to carry on their memory.

Indeed, for what future do we remember?

CHAPTER TWO

Going from Heirs to Founders: The Great Collective Narrative of Quebecers as Revisited by Gérard Bouchard

The situation in historiography in Quebec is very exciting. Many historians are returning to the great collective narrative of Quebecers of French-Canadian heritage, looking at it with rigour and openness.

This historical "revisionism," to employ the term used by Ronald Rudin,[1] was not born yesterday. It has been evident since the mid-1970s. It permeates the magnificent work by researchers at the CIEQ (Centre interuniversitaire d'études québécoises), who, in studying the basic morphologies of Quebec, have overturned the traditional view of Quebec as lagging behind economically and socially, and of the French Canadians as backward or out of step in their mentality and aspirations.[2] This "revisionism" is also discernable among those who, like Louis Rousseau and Frank Remiggi, are re-examining from another perspective the enduring importance of religion in Quebec in the nineteenth century, associating it with a broad movement of cultural revitalization that marked an entire society in search of solutions for the material and spiritual anxieties of a troubled time.[3] Even the Duplessis period, long seen as the antithesis of the Quiet Revolution, the quintessence of backwardness in terms of political conduct and forms of regulation, has been taken on and debunked by the new historians.[4]

It should be noted that the current questioning of the representations of Quebecers of French-Canadian heritage in the theatre of history is not the result of an exclusively empirical process. It also originates in a clear desire by certain authors to get away from a view of Quebec that they consider historically inadequate and politically inappropriate.[5]

By far the most prominent of these authors is Gérard Bouchard, who in the past twenty-odd years has carved out a prime place in the Quebec history establishment. The quality of his work and the scope of his investigations have enabled him to position himself as a major figure in the intellectual landscape of the province, indeed of Canada. Bouchard's scholarly activities have often had an impact in the public arena. He has frequently written scathing newspaper pieces in which he draws political conclusions based on his scholarly analyses.[6] He has published at least one article, in the magazine *L'Action nationale,* in which he attempted to give his theoretical reflections a more practical dimension.[7] In his recent popular novel, he has found a way to disseminate his theories and views to a public that is usually beyond the reach of academics.[8] In short, it would seem, given his influence and his many prestigious awards, that Gérard Bouchard is one of the potential heirs of that line of thinkers, from François-Xavier Garneau to Fernand Dumont, who have sought to nurture the historical consciousness of Quebecers, particularly those that used to be called French Canadians, by providing them with a great narrative – more or less edifying or melancholy – for them to tell themselves and others.[9]

Gérard Bouchard's relationship to his predecessors is one of both continuity and rupture. At first glance, what has been jettisoned is much more obvious than what has been kept. But, if we look more closely at his interpretative perspective in his most recent historical overviews, we discover that, in responding to the eternal desire for transcendence and re-foundation of Quebecers of French-Canadian heritage, which also figures in the thinking of his forebears, Bouchard remains stuck in an episteme in which the ideas of an *impediment to being* and a *deplorable lack of fulfillment* serve as the horizon against which he views his people's past and present.

In this piece, I will try, by going to the heart of his arguments, to bring to light the relationship between the scholarly and the political logic underlying Bouchard's theories on the "Quebec nation." Despite his distancing himself from the discourse of *la survivance*, Gérard Bouchard seems incapable of the difficult task of conceptualizing the identity of Quebecers in its constitutive ambivalences, its intermingled facets, its constant fits and starts. Like others before him, he is disconcerted by what he observes. He fails to grasp the Quebec collectivity in the structural and structuring tensions that have always constituted it. Instead of accepting the political consequences following from the recognition of these tensions, he attempts to remodel the past so as to neutralize its awkward ambiguities and turbulence. The problem, as one might imagine, does not lie in a lack of competence. It results, rather, from his understandable but questionable bias in favour of relevance, in favour of a dense, full history of the nation that would shore up the Quebec past against reality, against the infinite complexity of the banal and original actions of a population and cultures trying to prepare the way for themselves, with or against their prophets, in the shifting sands of the ordinary course of the world.

THE FOUNDATIONS OF THE BOUCHARDIAN PROJECT

To trace Gérard Bouchard's interpretative project with regard to the Quebec nation requires a clear grasp of the author's thinking on the role of history and historians in the production of meaning and the creation of social consensus.[10] It is on this scale and around these fundamental issues that he is most fully conscious of his role as an accomplished scholar. If, as a scholar, he wants to add to our knowledge of Quebec and open up thinking about Quebec society by "disorienting" it, his ultimate challenge is to discover the most appropriate way to rewrite the national past. The challenge is also to find the most accurate histori(ographi)cal definition of the collective *we*.[11] In other words, what Gérard Bouchard is concerned with is the creation of a renewed narrative of the origins of the community to which he belongs through socialization, choice, and empathy, a narrative that, as he himself says, is in keeping with the political and social boldness of the present time, that reconciles the Quebec experience with Americanness, that reflects the assurance Quebecers have finally found, that expresses the complexity of their collective life, and that takes up the challenge of a Quebec culture that is largely to be remade.[12]

Gérard Bouchard does not approach Quebec's past as a dilettante. He has earned his place and he acknowledges his commitments. The beginning and end point of his retroprospective quest is the "(sociological) Quebec nation."[13] While he acknowledges the danger, from a scholarly point of view, of abusing the concept of the nation and recognizes that "national history" as a specific genre entails significant methodological problems,[14] Bouchard chooses the nation as the central vector of Quebec's historical experience and the principal category for considering and restoring the meaning of that experience.[15] Although his position is justified on historical grounds, it is rooted more in a political option that overdetermines and skews his entire approach: that of the historical project of building an original francophone society on the territory of Quebec. Excluding any other interpretative consideration or option, Bouchard decides that it is not only legitimate, but desirable, judicious, and beneficial for the Quebec collectivity of today, the perceived nature of which provides a framework for his undertaking as a historian, to start from the idea and the reality of the Quebec nation in order to give a form to the past of this population that in the past or present became established in the space called Quebec and took part in its development.[16]

In Gérard Bouchard's interpretative project, there is thus a conscious attempt to find a *pertinent* common denominator – he himself speaks of a "paradigm" – on which to (re-)found the narrative of the origins of the Quebec collectivity. But this idea of a pertinent common denominator or paradigm is not self-evident. The choice of the most "appropriate" interpretative determinant here is Bouchard's. Given its inherent complexity and the inextricability of its registers and envelopes of meaning, the past does not possess any immanent or overriding capacity to impose its narrative forms. The pertinence of Bouchard's choice applies less to what the past of the inhabitants of Quebec actually was than to how the historian, as citizen and thinker, envisions the future of the community to which he belongs. This pertinence is essentially the reflection of a moral contract established between the intellectual and his society, a contract framed in terms of the most fruitful future to be created for his people. For Bouchard, the narrative of origins cannot be dissociated from the stakes involved in the extensive and inclusive (re)building of Quebec society.[17] He sees this narrative as – and wants it to be – a sort of wager tied to the blessed future of the nation, if not the (sovereign) state, of Quebec.[18]

And the key to the Bouchardian interpretative project may be found precisely in the future, in the horizon of meaning he is seeking to open for the members of his nation. Gérard Bouchard does not spend much time investigating the value of a national framework as the interpretive category and paradigm for the Quebec collectivity.[19] He makes it the postulate of his scholarly enterprise. Where necessary, he accepts its unfortunate and irremediable weaknesses on the pretext that, after all, the (civic) role of the discipline of history is to reduce the opacity of the past – and we know how anxiety-producing this opacity is.[20]

With this argument set forth, he establishes a few methodological principles in order to guide his peers in investigating the Quebec past in light of the (new) concept of the nation. These principles are as follows:

- first of all, to show the *we* in its transparency, to reveal it as it is in its positions, its instabilities, its successive transformations, always there but in movement;
- then, to avoid projecting this *we* as a given and thus writing teleology rather than history;
- finally, and especially, to re-envision the nation in a context of diversity so as to provide a foundation for collective cohesion that is as far as possible from ethnicity and is outside of ideological consensus or cultural homogeneity, while respecting beliefs and differences of all sorts.

For Gérard Bouchard, first for political and then historical reasons, there can be no Quebec history other than a national one, no history that does not focus on the experience of Quebec and Quebecers from the viewpoint of the emerging nation, a nation that is compared to a growing individual.[21] However, in this history of Quebec, the traditional tropes of Quebec history will be different. This history will be emphatically critical: it will have taken its distance from other, competing representations, in particular that of the survival of a cultural minority and that based on ethnic thinking, with its legitimization of the idea of the French-Canadian nation (or francophone Quebec nation), an idea Bouchard considers false, even dangerous.[22] Secondly, this national history will also be pluralistic: it will embrace all components of the nation, including new Quebecers, members of cultural communities, Amerindians, and anglophone Quebecers. Thirdly, this history will be objective: its partisans will not be afraid to speak of the pretences and subterfuges of the national imaginary, or of its contradictions, distortions, or omissions, even its abuses, violence, or other sins. This history will also be written from a universal and comparative perspective: the evolution of the Quebec nation will be considered and appraised in relation to the great processes of the establishment of societies, cultures, and other communities. The unique features of Quebec will thus be projected into an international context, which will make it possible to put them in perspective and at the same time to counter the ruses of the discourse on (and of) "Quebec exceptionalism."

In short, Gérard Bouchard's national history of Quebec will be that of a real country constituting itself in time, based on a full meaning, possessing its own centre of gravity, and aspiring to complete its four-hundred-year-long historical journey through its re-foundation in sovereignty.

While Bouchard denies that he is being anachronistic or teleological in rewriting the history of Quebec in the future perfect of the nation – although that is what is reflected in the title of one of his recent books, *La Nation québécoise au futur et au passé* [the Quebec nation in the future and the past] – and in making the past of his people a coherent or predictable thing shaped by an underlying structure, his claims seem vain when one goes to the heart of the epistemic system that gives rise to and structures his ideas.

THE (NEW) CIRCLE OF THE NATION

In spite of his having done important work based on primary data,[23] Gérard Bouchard is a historian who is not satisfied with empirical work; on the contrary, this is a scholar who is a master of the historical overview. He sees himself above all as the initiator of a project and the creator of an interpretative horizon. Gérard Bouchard opens up new areas, traces paths, orders questions in hierarchies, and suggests what in the panoply of research to be done is of first or secondary priority. Many of his texts are openly programmatic.[24] His role as a leading figure in the Quebec history establishment is hardly disputed. His followers and imitators are far more numerous than his critics.[25]

Gérard Bouchard is also a researcher tilling and surveying the ground of the past using implicit and explicit schematic models. The register of his writing may be concrete, but his arguments are firmly rooted in the great interpretative frameworks of a historiographical tradition brought to the United States by the proponents of historical sociology, the Braudelian school in France and the *Historische Sozialwissenschaft* movement in Germany.[26] This influence is clearly apparent in Bouchard's model for his project of reinterpreting the history of the Quebec nation. The model itself,[27] whose pertinence, according to Bouchard, goes well beyond the case of Quebec, is based on two central concepts, that of a "new collectivity" (or "founding culture") and that of "Americanness." For Bouchard, the societies of the New World (including Australasia and South Africa) have developed in a general pattern of continuity or rupture with the mother country, depending on various factors, but not merely as colonial enclaves; and this original orientation (continuity or rupture) had a decisive impact on their future development.

While he does not say so explicitly, Bouchard implies that rupture (or "reproduction in difference"), unlike the other option, that of continuity, has tended to have positive effects for populations becoming nations in that it led to a development marked by three successive, progressive phases of collective fulfillment: "appropriation" (historical consciousness), "new beginning" (utopian re-foundation), and "emancipation" (political re-foundation). Continuity, on the contrary, in a sense dried up the capacity of these populations to rise to complete nationhood by placing them in an uncomfortable duality, a cultural inconsistency, causing identity anxiety, confusion of being, and an inability to adopt lasting orientations.[28]

According to Bouchard's typology, the United States represents the classic case of a consummated rupture, complete disengagement, and successful reconnection.[29] "The history of the United States," he writes, "is quite clearly one of differentiation and rupture established through the War of Independence and accompanied by a very dynamic vision of a new collective beginning."[30] On the other hand, the republics of South America and Mexico, like Quebec and Canada, have, to varying degrees, stumbled over problems inherent in the great transition. These nations have shown themselves finally to be incapable of finding or creating that virtuous and so fondly desired balance between utopian and political re-foundation. The Latin-American countries are exemplary in this regard. According to Bouchard, these national cultures "succeeded in disengaging from their Iberian connection, but rather failed to make their American connection."[31] As for Australia and New Zealand, they present a completely different pattern of disengagement. There, while the model of differentiation and rupture eventually prevailed, the process took place in stages, with many ups and downs spread over a long period, and no definitive break. "The long duration of Australia's and New Zealand's disengagement from Great Britain," Bouchard says, "was such that it did not give rise to a discourse of triumphant, galvanizing rupture ... This leads to the paradox of two countries that have achieved political independence yet have not derived all the symbolic benefit from it."[32]

Seeking for a long time to reproduce the colonial imaginary, (English) Canada only disengaged very late and very gradually from Great Britain, and did so without a great founding act. Even now, the Canadian nation, incomplete in terms of a utopian vision and unable to shed the fear of being swallowed up by the Americans, has difficulty coming to terms with its desire for a rupture while seeking its identity in a distinctiveness that is in part invented.[33]

As for Quebec, burdened with a hundred years of false historical consciousness nurtured by a custodial Church and intellectuals frightened by the spectre of disappearance,[34] it has finally, happily, in the last fifty years, returned to the path of rupture. It has also come back to the road of emancipation in the utopianism of the Quiet Revolution and of sovereignty. Yet, paradoxically, this country always refuses to consummate its utopian re-foundation through the ultimate fulfillment of its quest for affirmation – political independence. This is why, according to Bouchard, Quebec in spite of everything remains an "old new country."[35] We can see that this question of the non-fulfillment of the nation through political independence haunts Gérard Bouchard. "How is it," he asks, "that, of all the [new] collectivities, Quebec is the only one [with Puerto Rico] that has not been able to achieve political independence?"[36]

Now, it is obvious that the past does not ask the historian this question of itself. This is a question that the interpreter, disappointed by his people's "broken" itinerary and continually "postponed" goal, addresses to the past. This heuristic reversal, which Bouchard claims is part of the historian's stock in trade,[37] is far from insignificant. Indeed, it makes it possible for him to put the dense, "disobedient," undefined material of the past back under the lens of the emerging nation, broken, diverted from its destiny, impeded from being, happily renewed, but still, alas!, in transition or in search of completion.

It is through this framework, which reinvents the question of *la survivance* by inscribing Quebec's history in the context of the objectified evolution of "new collectivities" and by reformulating it in terms of an impediment to being and a collective non-fulfillment, that Bouchard approaches the past of Quebec and Quebecers (of French-Canadian heritage). Similarly and accordingly, it is through this framework that he identifies the "depressing," rather than the founding, events of the community, structures the chapters of his history, and undertakes to build the new historical imaginary of his people.

In this undertaking, the comparative process is obviously crucial. Of course, comparativism gives historical analysis a dimension that may at times be beneficial, such as when it is used to expose and undermine "illusions of uniqueness."[38] The decision to stop studying Quebec in a vacuum, to abandon the outdated representation of a society with unique characteristics and a unique, even extraordinary, historical path, is one that, like many of my colleagues, I fully endorse. This said, comparativism is also very often used to evaluate and judge some cases in relation to others according to a general typology based on the identification – and idealization – of the most common case. Bouchard, while claiming to assiduously avoid such folly, indulges in this kind of "sententious comparativism," in which the success of processes in the past is judged on the basis of a supposedly objective model, when he places Quebec among the "new collectivities." Although the model he has developed is not without appeal from a formal point of view, it inevitably leads to arbitrary if not skewed judgments because of the questioning and historical analysis it gives rise to.

As I stated above, Bouchard sees the evolution of nations according to a general pattern of collective fulfillment that comprises three qualitative phases of transition or transformation of (collective-)Being-in-itself. And it is according to this objectified model that he assesses, compares, and classifies the cases he brings together: here, "rupture" has effectively been achieved; there, "appropriation" has been blocked; somewhere else, "re-foundation" has been thwarted or remains uncompleted. This is all well and good. But on the basis of what objective criteria can we speak of successful disengagement? What is a complete rupture? How can we evaluate whether or not a reconnection has been achieved? What is paradoxical about a collectivity not achieving sovereignty and not transcending itself in an independent state? What is the destiny that is eluded in one place and fulfilled in another? To what extent can a collectivity be classified as belonging to those that "go their own way" or to those that have advanced according to the "usual historical trajectory"?

Without recognizing it explicitly, Bouchard is seeking, through his model and his comparativism, to understand the particularities of the Quebec case in the light of other, related founding cultures – which, because new collectivities normally achieve sovereignty or else an explanation is required,[39] immediately places the province in a situation of historical "anomaly," or at least of irregularity or digression from its destiny in relation to a kind of universal that exists elsewhere, even incompletely.

The singularity of the Quebec nation, which is at the same time its misfortune and, certainly for Bouchard, the contradiction in its identity, is thus its not having won its political independence. From the Bouchardian perspective, the history of the Quebec nation is a narrative of lack and a call for a state (an independent state).

THE NARRATIVE OF LACK

The idea of the community having experienced a "digression from destiny" is crucial here. Gérard Bouchard's history of the nation is not the narrative of a people's dissidence or its innocence or its unconsciousness or its unconcern or its inconstancy or its apathy or its impotence or its latency. Nor is it a chronicle of a people or a culture facing and overcoming its ambivalence. It is essentially the narrative of a broken political project.[40]

In this narrative, there is a key event, not a definitive stop or an irrevocable reversal, but the suspension of a political itinerary that until then had proceeded more or less normally, that is, as a general movement of partial emancipation from the mother country (first phase in the Bouchardian model of "collective fulfillment").[41] That event is the insurrections of 1837–38, which were abortive or, rather, were violently repressed by the British.

Unlike the Conquest of 1759, which was sanctioned by the Cession of 1763 – a sequence of events that did not fundamentally change the situation for the population, which simply changed masters, Bouchard says – the rebellions were the culmination of political action that had begun at the turn of the century, whose goal was to establish a republic in Lower Canada. This action, which is a clear indication of the successful transition by the collectivity of Canadiens from "entity" to "identity" (the phases of "new beginning" and "appropriation" in Bouchard's model), was brutally stopped. The failure of the rebellions constituted nothing less than the diversion of the movement toward a rupture and re-founding, a movement that had started out normally but was thwarted at that point. This was followed by a long period of modification of the political dynamics of the French Canadians, a digression of their destiny from its *foreseeable* path (and from the "rupture" model favoured by Bouchard). This modification, directed by a Church that flaunted its loyalty to the Crown and then to Canada, was also supported by a large proportion of the educated people, who, abdicating the work on themselves that had been undertaken by a collectivity seeking its American path, developed a "false consciousness" – the term is Bouchard's – and kept the community in a position of withdrawal by binding it to the memory of *la survivance*. It would take a hundred years of guided "disappropriation" of the community by an intellectual class dependent on utopias of another time before the nation, kept in a state of hibernation in terms of its collective representations, would regain its initial momentum. The Quiet Revolution put the old Patriotes' dream of independence back on the agenda – permanently, according to Bouchard. It also brought part of the elite back to the path of rupture, placing the community back within the historical norm of "new collectivities." Hence Bouchard's enthusiasm for the current sovereignist movement, which he sees as the clear expression of a people in search of its founding act and finally laying down its status, if not its false identity, as heir.[42]

All things considered, the Bouchardian narrative of the contemporary evolution of Quebec is a narrative of a nation that, re-acknowledging its enduring historical nature in its regained desire for sovereignty (the ultimate stage of collective fulfillment, according to Bouchard), has finally recovered its rights with regard to its future. This view of Quebec's past at first glance appears somewhat reductive. However, the history (of the forced digression) of the Quebec nation that Gérard Bouchard is proposing is the result of a powerful interpretation by a brilliant and skillful narrator whose argument, wrapped in hope for the future, seduces and excites.[43] This interpretation draws on the most recent advances in the historiography of Quebec, to which Bouchard himself, as a researcher and former director of IREP (Institut interuniversitaire de recherches sur les populations), has contributed significantly.

It has been established over the last twenty years that the past of Quebec and Quebecers has not unfolded in suffering, affliction, narrowness of vision, and desire for withdrawal.[44] On the contrary, it is marked by many successes. In economic and social terms in particular, the development of the Quebec collectivity has been quite similar to that of other fringe or frontier societies; its particularities are the result of the way the population appropriated its space, coping with the constraints of its physical and economic environment rather than merely submitting to them.[45] Similarly, it is inaccurate to suggest that modernity came to Quebec only belatedly. The truth is that Quebec's Americanness has always been a source of modernity.[46] In a word, the evolution of Quebec has been "normal." In the beginning and even later, Quebec society was and saw itself potentially as no different from others.

It is this optimistic, confident perspective that serves as the postulate of Gérard Bouchard's histori(ographi)cal undertaking. The vision underlying it is strong and effective: like a child that has every advantage, Quebec, like many other "new collectivities," possessed the capacity to re-found itself through "inscription" rather than "prescription," that is, as a full political nation rather than as an entity subordinated to a larger whole. However, this predisposition was not realized. The question Bouchard then places at the heart of his investigation is the following: how can the absence – at least until now – of a political (re-)foundation of the "Quebec nation" be explained?

Note the subtle shift of the line of inquiry: it is not so much a matter of explaining why Quebec *did* positively evolve in a particular direction – and conceptualizing, acknowledging, or endorsing the uniqueness of that original and acceptable itinerary[47] – as of grasping why it *did not,* for a long time, evolve in the expected direction, until it recently recovered, only to hesitate again to finally fulfill itself. Gérard Bouchard's whole interpretative project is framed around this question, which is loaded and overdetermined by the negative idea of Quebec's incompletion, a kind of failed or unfulfilled state of collective existence resulting largely, according to him, from Quebecers' difficulty in perceiving and projecting themselves as an entity and from their sorrow at their rupture with their French and European references in order to constitute themselves as an original society on the new continent.[48] According to his logic, Quebecers' tragedy results largely from their inability to adopt a new attitude with regard to identity and their difficulty in tearing themselves away from themselves.[49]

In this, there is no doubt that Gérard Bouchard's vision of Quebec's historical experience is imbued with a perennial melancholy that other thinkers before him have sustained in memorable turns of phrase. He seems wounded by the direction and the outcome of his people's past *in comparison to what that past could have been.* Most of all, he refuses to acknowledge the meaning of that past – which would in his view be to accept the inevitability of what has been – or to acknowledge in his narrative what he sees as the community's regrettable non-fulfillment – regrettable in that it is the outcome of one of many scenarios *that did not come to pass.*[50] Despite the reservations one is entitled to have with respect to counterfactuality as an intellectual approach, one should not be surprised here by Bouchard's position as a scholar: to him, "reflection on non-events is [also] part of historical research."[51]

This said, Bouchard does not reproduce pre-existing arguments to express his "homesickness" for his country. He tries, rather, to update a narrative whose tropes are unsuited to him, and from which he wants to distance himself. He does not place his interpretative project within the paradigm of *la survivance,* but within that of emergence. His ambition is not to protect the community from assault by others or from the sufferings of elsewhere by putting it back on a horizon of weak continuity and withdrawal. His ambition is to guide his people in the final emancipation of their historical consciousness by redeeming their itinerary through a narrative of collective advancement under the aegis of three determinants of identity: the civic ideal of recognition and tolerance, the acknowledgment of the constitutive heterogeneity of the Quebec collectivity, and the experience of building an original francophone community in North America.[52]

Gérard Bouchard's aim is, through the discipline of history, to nurture and support the new movement toward rupture that he perceives in Quebecers (of French-Canadian heritage). In doing so, he is seeking to become one with his people in transcending their past. Like Serge Cantin and many others, he chooses to support his country as one does a child – a moral propensity of the (francophone) Quebec intellectual that I will discuss below.

Using the paradigm of emergence to (re)think Quebec's past, Bouchard builds his argument in four stages that are logically connected through two key events: the rebellions of 1837–38 and the Quiet Revolution.[53] It should be noted that both these events involved – but in different power relationships and reverse situations – the same adversaries, the central "characters" in the traditional narrative of Quebec history: not francophones and anglophones, or even Quebecers and Canadians, but the forces of Progress and Emancipation (whose courage he salutes) and the forces of Stagnation and Impediment (which he vilifies). In this history that he composes as though it were the opera of his people's identity and he the maestro, Bouchard presents the forces of Stagnation as the victors over the forces of Progress in the first event, in the mid-nineteenth century. One hundred years later, the opposite outcome occurred. In both cases, the national space of Quebec is seen as the theatre in which universal struggles take place that are in no way sectarian or unique and that feature the typical actors of modernity – on one side, virtuous, on the other, pitiful – striving to give their heirs a legacy of progress forward or movement backward.

This, it may be noted, is a fashionable reformulation, in keeping with the political generosity and the post-ethnic ideals of our time, of one of the most powerful mechanisms in the formation of the Quebec collectivity, namely the conflict, or at least the tension, between francophone Quebecers (formerly French Canadians) and the other cultures that make up the Quebec collectivity.[54]

Be that as it may, let us look at Bouchard's narrative, which is completely organized in terms of the national hypothesis:

- In the beginning – a kind of "year zero" in collective life – there was a nucleus of French immigrants who, while appropriating the contributions of the communities that surrounded them, the Amerindians in particular, gradually became involved in a general, quiet movement toward partial emancipation from the mother country. The Conquest and the trauma it caused in the local population did not end this profound process of disengagement and rupture. On the contrary, the affirmation of identity by the Canadiens, who were expressing an embryonic but firm desire for a new beginning in Americanness, was strengthened against this "other," the colonial administration, which persisted in handling the development of the colony as part of the political economy of the metropolis. From that time on, and more and more intensely and openly, the situation of Here was countered by that of Elsewhere. It was in this context that a living national feeling began to emerge among the Canadiens – the "prehistory" of "We Quebecers."
- The insurrections of 1837–38 were a major turning point in the process of affirmation that had begun, taking the emerging nation back to its starting point.[55] The democratic desire clearly expressed by "people from Here" – primarily francophones, but anglophones, too – for a collective refounding in a liberal, secular, and autonomous republican state was thwarted by "people from Elsewhere." The banning of the Parti Patriote, combined with the constitutional

reprimands that followed the insurrections, impeded the self-reappropriation that could have led to the project of an independent state, both sanction and herald of a happy new beginning for the nation in tune with the continental dream, triumphant liberalism, and emerging civil society.[56]

- At this point, the community's progress was diverted, and the "new" collectivity gradually adopted the reflexes of an "old society." It stagnated, mainly because its educated people and interpreters refused or were unable to name the country and proved themselves poor trustees of the emerging national feeling. Accepting rather than trying to overcome the impasses in which the nation found itself, and thus impeding its development, they condemned it to bare survival and marginalization. Gradually, a mythic memory of origins replaced the excitement of the American dream: the future was blocked, and the society seemed stuck. Caught between the false self-consciousness offered by its intellectual class, on the one hand, and its inability to express its persistent but discouraged Americanness in original cultural forms, on the other, the people, for want of an alternative, assimilated a national reference that destroyed its potential for emancipation and brought it back to a state of withdrawal completely centred on the idea of continuity as the path to collective transcendence. This was the beginning of an unfortunate diversion of Quebec's destiny in relation to that of similar societies in America. Its manifestations of self-assertion, directed toward the ideal of continuity, caused it to sink more deeply into a perilous horizon fed by equivocal thinking. Quebec thus survived divided from itself. Broken by the other that prevented it from politically and symbolically cutting its European ties, the Quebec people, from the mid-nineteenth century on, was inhibited by its clergy, which, drugged on the abstract idea of the greatness of France, gave it a voice that contradicted and suppressed the authentically American and thoroughly modern characteristics of its objective existence. At the cost of falsification of its urban, heterogeneous reality and denial of its original, hybridized forms of cultural expression, the community was thus brought back into the orbit of continuity (a deplorable option to Bouchard), a deviation from its historical path. A functional but harmful division between the body and the spirit of the nation, an internal alienation, was created that was to last a hundred years. In terms of its overall representations, Quebec was masquerading in garments of questionable taste.

- The evil spell of continuity was lifted (but not completely removed) when new heralds of Enlightenment cast another spell on the people with the freshness and pertinence of their interpretations, articulating more appropriate collective representations. The people was resuscitated and the nation revived. For Bouchard, the Quiet Revolution marked the newly rejuvenated collectivity's acquisition of a historical consciousness worthy of it. The nation finally emerged from its long silence. It was able to rediscover and once more express its constitutive and unalterable Americanness. This reversal of perspective in many respects saved the Quebec collectivity. With the Quiet Revolution, it undertook to reinvent itself as a culture with its own distinctive features, articulating an emergent Quebec Americanness, rather than a culture of borrowings, the pale extension of a Europeanness in a state of extraterritorial drift.[57] This process of collective redefinition reflects the return of the nation to a trajectory of rupture, disengagement, and continental utopianism, the expected culmination of which is a new beginning in independence. Starting again where it had been stopped, and finally freed of the false consciousness in which it was encapsulated, the Quebec nation is able, if its leaders and participants so desire, once and for all to acknowledge its identity and, as its sisters have done before it, to attain triumphant Americanness. Finally the Quebec collectivity is able to go from heir to founder. However, to Bouchard's great displeasure, this desire for emergence remains suspended on the horizon and fails to materialize in the form of a project of political independence.

It is with this conclusion, a surprising one in terms of the narrative that supports it, and a painful one for him, that Gérard Bouchard's argument is left stranded. In light of his view that the winning conditions exist for Quebecers to finally achieve their continental dream, it is indeed difficult to understand how it is that they continue to hesitate to make the decision.

Even though this hesitation cannot, for him, be conceptualized as a *place of being*, but only condemned as a *paradox of identity*, the only way out for Bouchard is to insist that today's Quebecers still have those unfortunate reflexes and complexes associated with false consciousness and false representation created by the clergy of old. And this, in fact, is the direction he takes, following the many authors before him who did not hesitate to use more or less veiled culturalist interpretations to explain the "depressing ambiguity" of Quebecers (of French-Canadian heritage). Rather than instructing us on the complex and indeterminate reality of the past, these culturalist explanations reflect their narrators' abdication of the task of elucidating what is obvious but that they do not necessarily want to see or to reveal for reasons of the political pertinence of their narratives.

This intellectual abdication when confronted with the complexity of things – an attitude that should not be condemned *ex cathedra* – is characteristic of Gérard Bouchard's interpretative project. His narrative is not primarily a comprehensive, explanatory thesis on the complicated but original itinerary of a community of history and memory that formed empirically in the past and is seeking, through a pragmatic politics, to discover the most accommodating option of the time in order to continue its march with and against its changing partners. Rather, it is a narrative whose aim is to *redeem* the inhabitants of Quebec of yesterday and today by presenting them as an emerging nation in movement against its external "impeders," the gravediggers of its true consciousness, and, finally, against itself in its exasperating ambivalence of being.

THE NA(RRA)TION OF REDEMPTION AND UNIVERSALISM

To properly assess Gérard Bouchard's scholarly contribution, it is necessary to make a distinction between his empirical historical works and his overviews. The former are absolutely remarkable. No one who seriously studies Quebec society and seeks to understand its morphological aspects and contours can ignore his major contribution; this is especially true of his work on society in the Saguenay region.

His overviews, on the other hand, particularly the most recent ones, show a surprising simplicity of vision with respect to the central and overall dynamics of Quebec's historical experience. Not that the man has lost his interpretive powers, but rather, I would say, that he refuses, out of political conviction and concern, to draw the conclusions from what he observes in the material of the past. This refusal is expressed in the use of the concept of paradox in order to think, or rather not to think – which is different from "unthinking," and I will come back to this – the constitutive "connections" in what was, and still is in many ways, the experience of (francophone) Quebec on North-American soil.

The concept of paradox, like that of ambiguity, allows Bouchard to circumvent the difficulty of conceptualizing what is ambivalent, contradictory, or hard to explain in the fulfillment of the past but, for reasons that belong not to the past but to the history we make of it or the political project that history supports, cannot be left in such a deplorable state of incompletion[58] or interpretative irresolution and approximation. To say that an attitude is paradoxical is, in the case of a rational person, to imply that it goes against the common sense of its prior trajectory and that the person has digressed from the objective and expected conditions of development. On the scale of a collectivity that is considered sound, a paradoxical attitude means the community's actions do not correspond to the order of the narrative as defined by the narrator. Clearly, the paradox is not that of the community, which is seeking its path in the ongoing flow of events, in a situation of constant malaise and irreducible tensions. Rather, the paradox results from the intellectual approach of the narrator, who, a prisoner of the aporias of his vision, embarks on an interpretation that leads to a dead end because of the specious reasoning used.

And Gérard Bouchard's interpretative project does indeed appear to be based on an aporia – that of the previous and present existence of the "Quebec nation" – of which he is perfectly aware but which he has decided to take to the bitter end. The lucidity he demonstrates with regard to the central contradiction of his interpretation – he actually speaks of a "wager" on the present and the future – is expressed even more explicitly in his question, How can one, drawing on historical scholarship, project into the past a collective cohesion that is not found in the present – and, I would add, that was no more evident in the past?[59] In other words, is it possible, and is it justified from a scholarly point of view, to represent the Quebec past from the perspective of a history of the nation in Bouchard's sense, that is, as a political and historical community that is all-encompassing in terms of identity?

Intellectual rigour and simple respect for Quebec history demand a negative answer to this question – a lucid conclusion that Fernand Dumont had already reached, with a certain regret although without spleen.[60] Although drawing on a different courage and appealing to a higher imperative, Bouchard denies this assessment and proposes to substitute for the sometimes discouraging and inadequate reason of scholarship, the more utopian but in his eyes indispensable reason of the new political community to be built.

For Bouchard, the wager of the historian as intellectual and citizen is to respect his obligations to the present and take the consequences in terms of his arguments. Clearly, the discipline of history cannot deny its responsibility to help lay the foundations for consensus and give society a new direction.[61] It seems that to Bouchard this responsibility is complementary to the scholarly enterprise. In fact, he sees nothing wrong with making history contribute to the creation of culture. Does he not point out that the imperative of identity and nation is the one that, intentionally or not, historiographies inevitably end up being enlisted to serve as part of their duty to create social and political cohesion rather than dissension or indecision? For Bouchard, a scholarly approach is in fact measured by the coherence of the connections to which knowledge gives rise (the principle of demonstration), from the perspective of the explicit premises on which it is based (the principle of interpretation). In this, Gérard Bouchard openly shows his colours. He writes:

> The model of the Quebec nation is still the one that opens up the richest perspectives for our society; it is also the one that makes it possible to avoid or to resolve the most difficulties while reconciling the imperatives of law, sociology, and history. [This model] affirms the possibility in Quebec of a cultural nation superimposed on the civic nation (or the people). It fosters respect for diversity, social cohesion, and the struggle against discrimination. It advocates an original configuration that is based on the most progressive classical models or ideal types while reflecting the situation and aspirations of Quebec today. Finally, it suggests essentially a redefinition, a broadening of the collective *we*, no longer associating it with French Canadians but with all of francophone Quebec.[62]

Here we get to the bottom of Gérard Bouchard's interpretative project and historiographical program: to rebuild the Quebec nation, to bring it together, despite its more or less structural dissensions and dispersions, in one sublime, salutary, and liberating idea of a North American francophone collectivity that is motivated and driven forward by a project of collective development. It is in this sense that I speak of Bouchard's narrative enterprise as an attempt to redeem the community through collective transcendence and re-foundation.

It would be easy to demonstrate through a close analysis of Bouchard's historical overviews how, in his desire to fulfill the political responsibility he has taken on for the benefit of those he loves, he strives to systematically redeem Quebec's past in a history of collective salvation. It is in relation to this redemptive purpose that one has to understand his efforts to present the Native peoples as the first Quebecers and not just the original inhabitants of the territory of Quebec, to neutralize the ethnic prism through which Quebec's history has primarily been seen until now, to untie the knot of collective legacies and "false representations" of Quebecers by rewriting their "identity equation" according to the formula $Q = -F + GB + USA^2 - R$,[63] to include in the idea of the nation all the cultural components of the collectivity of Quebec as if everything that has happened in the territory of Quebec had to do with the nation, to exclude from the national history what might remain of resentment and aggression in the French-Canadian memory, and so on.

While drawing on a historical vision that he describes as broad, inclusive, and generous – which I do not dispute, and which is greatly to his credit – Gérard Bouchard appears to be trapped in a model that, although it fits well with his utopian ideal, does not jibe with the past as it was or the present as it is. In fact, he seems dismayed, even bewildered, by what he observes in his nation today. He makes two pathetic observations:

First of all, after a half-century of quiet revolution, Quebec still seems, regrettably, to be in transition; its future has even become uncertain. There are several indications of this: the old French-Canadian identity is undergoing a resurgence; anglophone Quebecers are resistant to a national project they have always seen as suspect and that, it must be admitted, "has become a little ambiguous"; Amerindians are asserting their own desire for autonomy; immigrant Quebecers are divided, with many integrating into the anglophone linguistic community and most joining the Canadian nation.[64]

Second, and even more worrying, is the fact that old conceptions of the nation are reappearing, opening the door to a return to ethnic thinking. These conceptions, which have been expressed by influential thinkers, among them even Fernand Dumont, stress the indelible nature of the French-Canadian (or francophone Quebec) reference in the articulation of a vision of the future for the collectivity. According to these views, which Bouchard sharply criticizes, the horizon of Quebec cannot – except for purposes of partisan mystification, of which sovereignty is only one variant – be separated from the promotion of the francophone community, which is a full-fledged nation.[65] What is to be done under the circumstances?

Given the problems of collective reciprocity and reconciliation that he sees in the Quebec political arena, and the obsolete views that he sees as incarnations of the old syndrome of *la survivance* and that he fears could lead to a dead end and irreparable alienation for the Quebec collectivity, Bouchard chooses, as a conscientious citizen and responsible scholar, to invest his energies in getting the collective identity back in shape. Rather than remain silent and await the final disenchantment with the idea of the nation or redefine it on an ethnic basis and thus see Quebec end up in an impasse, Gérard Bouchard prefers to put his faith in another enterprise, one he considers eminently legitimate and useful for the future: [66] reformulating the nation in terms of diversity.

How far is he ready to go to support and sustain this "exciting challenge, this project of openness, this work of civilization" that drives his historiographical quest and civic commitment? Very far, it seems: in the direction of the past, as we have seen, as far as rethinking the collectivity in terms of the nation, by including all social affiliations, even if they are quite foreign to the national focus, in the overall framework of a political community that he considers equivalent to the (unfortunately not sovereign) nation; in the direction of the present, as he writes in a stinging article, as far as throwing into the Saint-Jean-Baptiste Day bonfire all the old stock cluttering the place of the nation, in the hope that a renewed and enriched species of Quebecer will be born out of the ashes.[67]

An offering to the future of his people, Gérard Bouchard's na(rra)tion of redemption is intended as nothing less than a work of historical catharsis in favour of a new collective universalism. It is in this light that his work should be assessed.

CRITIQUE OF THE BOUCHARDIAN PROJECT

To avoid any misunderstanding, let me state clearly that it would be a mistake to condemn Gérard Bouchard's intellectual enterprise in its entirety. He takes full responsibility as a narrator, and he seeks to establish a positive relationship between a representation of the historical path of the Quebec collectivity, which path he defines as the space of the nation's experience, and the utopian vision that governs his approach as a historian, that is, the horizon of expectation that inspires him and in relation to which he situates himself as a thinking and acting subject. Of course, the simplicity of his interpretation and the slanted use of his method of comparativism are disappointing. But that is not the most glaring problem.

I readily admit that the interpretative act must be limited, on one hand, by the facts – a constraint I recognize as unavoidable – and, on the other hand, by the need to create a coherent account – a goal I consider desirable, even indispensable. In the Bouchardian project, however, it seems that the balance between the scholarly value of the interpretation and its political virtue is flawed. Not only is the past co-opted to serve a constraining and in the end simplistic definition of the issues, but the utopian ideal does not seem very realistic in relation to a pragmatic position that takes into account the historical axes that have structured the Quebec collectivity. In short, the Bouchardian history of the nation does not link remembering with becoming in a fruitful way for the Quebec collectivity of yesterday and today. It is for this reason, first and foremost, that I consider it pertinent to criticize his views.

That does not, of course, mean that all his propositions should be rejected. For example, his suggestion that the whole question of relations between Native peoples and non-Natives in the colonial era be re-examined in light of the view of the latter as invaders seems fully justified. However, to go from there to considering the Native peoples as the original inhabitants *of Quebec,* and even as the first *Quebecers,* and to begin the history of this collectivity with the Indian and Inuit immigrations to North America, is a leap that simple scholarly rigour should not allow. It is also an interpretative presumption that the lucid observation of contemporary Quebec society in no way justifies. One may want the Native communities, along with other communities, to be part of the Quebec (or Canadian) collectivity; one may also, with this goal in mind, seek histori(ographi)cal ways to adapt the national idea to the imperative of Quebec's (or Canada's) ethnic and cultural diversity, favouring integration over difference and disharmony; but one must be well aware that to do so involves a *political wager* that the past does not readily support and that the present only allows in a limited way.[68] From this point of view, it seems that, in the desire not to be driven by the past, Gérard Bouchard is imprudently distancing himself too far from it; this does not appear to be a satisfactory solution.

The facts of the past, in their irreducible complexity, provide a much more confused, uncertain, and discordant image of relationships between Native peoples and non-Natives. While it is possible to cite exchanges, borrowings, partial adaptations, and mutual compromises by these two "generic cultures" that met in a the space of economic and social relations, and while it is perfectly appropriate to emphasize the real assimilation, by both Natives and non-Natives, of elements, objects, rituals, and symbols belonging to the "other," this in no way means that there was a convergence or an accommodation or any desire to bring the two cultures closer together.[69] In fact, it is the opposite that occurred: the domination and exclusion of the Native peoples by the non-Natives.[70]

Despite their constant interaction, the two communities have largely evolved in their separate ways, and have done so in a relationship of sometimes constructive, sometimes negative tensions. This should not be surprising. History teaches us that, rather than mixing together in hybrid unions, cultures appropriate contributions from outside through interactions of all kinds, and assimilate them, merging them into their own cosmologies.[71] This was certainly the case for the Native peoples and non-Natives that coexisted in the St Lawrence Valley.[72]

We may then ask ourselves whether it is preferable, in order to build the future and found the new "Quebec nation," to establish a symbolic line of descent between Native peoples and non-Natives, considering the former the ancestors of the latter – a kind of retroactive hybridization of memory that seems rather extreme[73] – or whether it would be better to acknowledge that the communities largely evolved in distinct, though not impervious, worlds, establishing their relationship as neighbours on the basis of interactions of co-operation and antagonism from which it was possible, by lucidly accepting the existence of this double bind, to extract a capital of plenitude rather than harm, and to do so in order to build a future made up of reparations, compromises, and alliances acceptable to all. Obviously, we must be very conscious of the possibilities and lines of thinking each of the options gives rise to.

In the first case – which permits contemporaries to free themselves from the irreparable wounds of history – the past is reviewed and corrected on the horizon of the utopian vision of co-integration, the present is "conjugated" in the future perfect of the nation, and becoming takes primacy over remembering. There is only one outcome politically: the refoundation of Quebec, a revolution of hearts and minds, the rebirth of Quebec and Quebecers through the embellishment and lamination of the past – in short, a totally new beginning in the national ideal.

In the second case – which presupposes that the descendants not only recognize what has been but also distance themselves from it – there is a critical acceptance of the factuality of the past, but not of its enduring nature; that is, there is an acceptance of an unalterable "precipitate" left by the effects of human life in space and time – namely, distinctive cultures – but there is also, *on this basis,* a responsible moral quest for narrative and societal arrangements that are favourable, positive, and productive for the present and future and also compatible with a subtle, rigorous, and complete reading of the past. Politically, the choice is clear: society constantly enriches itself through trial and error, pragmatism, compromise, accommodation, change, and improvement. The assumptions underlying this overall progress seem obvious: revolution, re-foundation, and new beginnings are not the only way to improvement; rebirth is not always needed to bring about what seems right and good; Quebec society is not currently in an identity crisis; every wound has its appropriate healing.

As one might imagine, Bouchard's reinterpretive project is not limited to the revision of the relationship between Native peoples and non-Natives. It also bears on the nature of the ties among the linguistic and cultural communities that have lived and developed in the territory of Quebec. His aim here, as in the case of the Native peoples, is to overturn the accepted interpretation. It is no more or less than to reshape the face of the nation and to review its narrative by the standard of diversity and universality as opposed to that of ethnicity and survival. It is, even more, by enlarging the circle of the nation to its maximum extension, to include and integrate, in the place of the na(rra)tion, all the actors, all the communities, all the cultures and ethnic groups, and all the segments that have formed the Quebec collectivity, yesterday and today.

Of course, Bouchard does not take issue with the idea of a multiplicity of communities living and renewing themselves in Quebec. At the same time, he does not want to diminish the historical tragedy experienced by francophone Quebecers.[74] That being said, he is sensitive to the need to break out of the apparent deadlocks of the past, which he feels have led to a hardening of identities, and he has no intention of making the thesis of cultures in tension a structural element of his history of the collectivity. In the Bouchardian narrative, there is no longer one ethnic group (or one culture) against another. There is instead a general collectivity that struggles against the imperialist trusteeship to which it has been subjected for a long time, including the period of the French regime.[75] There is also a whole collectivity that is seeking to build its Americanness as an actor shaping its destiny here and not as the heir of goals from elsewhere. There is, finally, a more focused collectivity that, while marked by internal disputes of an ethnic nature, has nevertheless always worked toward co-integration, not merely coexistence, and even less cohabitation.

Here again, Bouchard's critical judgment and scholarly reflexes seem to have been swept away by the therapeutic goals of his interpretation and the political ideology driving his civic project. Not only does he wrongly neutralize an element that is a constant (although it is continually resolved or subsumed) in Quebec's past, namely the tension in the relationship between francophones and other Quebecers, but he also tries to diminish the density of the internal differences, separations, and discordances in the "national collectivity" in favour of its external lines of demarcation and distinction.

In the Bouchardian view of the francophone Quebec collectivity, the line of identity defining and circumscribing the community is absolutely clear: on one side are *We (all) Quebecers;* on the other are those people who do not belong to this *We* for reasons of extraterritoriality, lack of sympathy toward the Quebec nation, or self-exclusion. It is through the reification and consecration of the Whole against its "disobedient" constituent parts and "internal rebels" (those elements that seek deliberately to "exclude" themselves from the nation) and in relation to its external adversaries or partners that Gérard Bouchard delimits the place of the Quebec nation.[76] However, this place is largely artificial. It has meaning only in terms of the horizon expected by the historian – the formation of a sovereign political community founded on the idea of an open francophone collectivity, Quebec culture, and a project of collective development – and not in terms of the actual experience of the actors, as a territory where, for a long time or since more recently, communities of culture have been living and renewing themselves, influencing each other in the spontaneous and unpredictable transactions of everyday life, interacting in happiness, weariness, or pain, depending on the circumstances, but in no way denying their specific ties and places of memory, many of which are outside the national territory. Must we see this quiet pragmatism and the recognition of it intellectually and politically as misery, resignation, and withdrawal or as catastrophe in the making, as Bouchard seems to feel?

Gérard Bouchard is making a wager on the nation, or rather on this new nation he discerns in its emergent fragility, seeking to make of the past something other than what the past has made of Quebec, as if the current situation in the province were tragic or were moving toward a dead end. However, contrary to what he would like, he must nonetheless observe that contemporary Quebec remains largely a product of its history – which is one of ambivalence of being and crossed ties – a situation that its inhabitants, the francophone majority first and foremost, learned to deal with quite a while ago and know how to turn to advantage while finding secure refuge in it.

According to some people, dealing with this situation has meant that francophone Quebecers, the former French Canadians, suffer from a complex of the colonized.[77] I would say that it has more to do with the destiny of a linguistic minority that has developed on a continental scale beside a hegemonic culture, and that has been able to continue to exist and to thrive by combining reflective wisdom with the skillful practice of pragmatic politics. This minority, which is a majority within a clearly circumscribed territory in Canada – Quebec – undeniably forms a community of memory, history, and culture that is distinctive in relation to other Quebec communities and even more so to francophone communities in the rest of Canada. It also possesses – and this is no small thing – direct, full access to a state apparatus, be it "truncated" or "amputated" as is often said, which enables it to have a voice and to express its identity through institutional means. And this minority is – the third characteristic – an integral part (in fact the major component) of the Quebec collectivity, which in turn is a constitutive element of the larger established collectivity that is Canada. The Quebec collectivity exists as the historical coming together of communities that, while living side by side, tend to reproduce themselves, exchanging with each other without melting into an indistinct or engulfing cultural mass. Together, these communities, which practise an enviable mutual tolerance and have very rarely expressed their differences in ethnic conflict, provide ideas and projects to nourish a common public space where all can express their individuality or affiliation with a group or a community of belonging, and state their views. These views are endorsed – or not – by the government, which translates them into legal forms appropriate for a political community (which could also be called the civil collectivity) dependent on and entrusted with representative democracy and the individual and collective welfare of its members.

What I call the Quebec collectivity could very well be called a "nation." In practice, this hardly matters sociologically. But it is important to be aware that the "nation" seen in this way is nothing more than a general political entity that does not transcend its constitutive cultural differences (Must these cultures be called "sub-nations"?),[78] nor does it recognize itself exclusively in the generic idea of a francophone collectivity, nor does it use the term "nation" to represent itself entirely when it expresses itself in its constitutive and integrative totality. The "nation of Quebec," if one absolutely insists on this concept, refers to the community of francophones of French-Canadian heritage and those "assimilated" into this community. To claim the opposite today is, at the very least, to show evidence of error and illusion rather than lucidity.[79]

However, Gérard Bouchard does not want to accept this reality of the Quebec collectivity, which is a relativization of the idea of the "Quebec nation." To him, the idea of francophone Quebec (or French-Canadian) culture belongs to an ethnographic or a substantialist conception of human groups. He is wrong. The structuring of the Quebec collectivity – as of the vast majority of collectivities in the world – in terms of ethnicity is an unavoidable sociological fact that does not necessarily present a problem. Moreover, the cultures that meet in fruitful exchanges in the territory of Quebec and continually reaffirm and reshape their identities, their heritages, and their ideals make the cultural space of Quebec a place of freedoms and differences that should be preserved and protected. In fact, Quebec culture – in my perspective, the varied culture that exists in the social entity of Quebec – has for a long time been (and will continue for a long time to be) the product of a creative double tension between hybridities and lines of descent, on the one hand, and between centripetal forces (everything that tends toward a shared framework) and centrifugal forces (everything that tends toward diversification), on the other hand. There is no doubt that this double tension should be maintained. It is on this condition alone, as Bouchard himself asserts, that the coexistence ("cohabitation" in my vocabulary) of disparate cultural components can translate into creativity and true enrichment for everyone.[80]

Of course, it may be that the recognition of the unavoidable and invigorating ethnic composition of the population of the territory of Quebec poses a problem for the achievement of Quebec sovereignty. But is it a problem for the future of the Quebec collectivity? And is it a problem for the progress of the community the francophones of Quebec comprise? And is it a problem for the welfare and happiness of those people who see themselves as part of this community? To answer these questions in the affirmative, as Gérard Bouchard does, is to express a political bias that cannot easily be camouflaged in the language of history. In my view, this partisan perspective is the foundation of Bouchard's interpretative edifice. His words suggest there is a problem in the Quebec collectivity not being exclusively a nation, or in the "(francophone) Quebec nation" not being perfectly congruent with the Quebec collectivity. If such a problem exists, it is in my opinion more because of Bouchard's political options than the actual or latent tragedy of Quebec.

In the conscious refusal to endorse the direction of the past and present experience of his people may be found both the crux and the impasse of the Bouchardian intellectual project: Why is it necessary at all costs to discover, found, incite, and create the nation if the majority of Quebecers, francophones included, adapt quite well, though with an ambivalence of heart and mind that is a tradition for them, to the *modus vivendi* and *modus operandi* within and outside their place of being? Are ambivalence and cohabitation in tension with the "other" necessarily suicidal options for the community, an abdication of the task to be accomplished, a rejection of the utopian solidarity? Could it not be, rather, that they express a certain reflective wisdom – a wisdom tested by the ancestors and bequeathed to their descendants – in the building of a present and a future along the felicitous line of pragmatism, mutual respect for cultures, and friendship?

It is not my intention here to return to a debate that goes far beyond the scope of this chapter. It may be thought that Bouchard's quest for a political nation, which is shored up by the existence of a cultural nation that he wants to see transcend itself in an epiphany of otherness, "stateness," and sovereignty arises from his model, described above, of the ultimate fulfillment of (collective)-Being-in-itself, a fulfillment that comes about through the completion of the original community in the sovereign state. It is clear that to Bouchard gaining political independence would enable Quebecers, and Quebecers of French-Canadian heritage in particular, to realize themselves once and for all, that is, to finally cease surviving and instead develop fully as a responsible francophone nation and society.

Underlying this argument is a utopian vision of re-foundation that is a powerful element of the French-Canadian imaginary, and that, with other elements, has for a very long time inspired a quest for affirmation. There is also a desire for formal political representation in the great scheme of contemporary states – which is certainly legitimate, but which is not justified very well by the proponents of sovereignty. And finally, hidden behind this argument is the malaise of an intellectual who has become impatient with waiting for his own collectivity to emerge from its reputed ambiguity – and its "equivocal thinking" – to surge forward in a definitive reconquest of itself.

Gérard Bouchard's goal is to break the circularity of Quebec and transform Quebecers from heirs to founders, as if the development of the Quebec collectivity were stuck in *la survivance*. To search his intellectual project for an appropriate avenue for fully apprehending the past of the Quebec collectivity and envisioning its future is to search in vain.

CHAPTER THREE

What History for the Future of Canada?

There is an issue that will loom on the horizon of Canada in the twenty-first century: that of the great collective narrative on which the vision of the country will be built – if indeed a vision of this country is thinkable and a narrative possible. I believe such a vision is thinkable, such a narrative is possible, and both are desirable.[1]

At the present time, the visions and narratives of the past circulating in the public arena have proven to be more negative than positive for preparing a happy future for the country. Most of the efforts to resolve the structural conflicts and disagreements that mark the entity of Canada are directed toward the political and constitutional sphere. The scholarly sphere of history, whose importance in reopening the future of Canada in a fruitful way has been underestimated, is largely neglected.[2] The political powers are involved, of course, but they are interested in trendy representations of Canadian history that "strengthen and celebrate Canada."[3] The intellectual community seems to be having a good deal of difficulty forging a narrative of mediation and conciliation, rather than of separation, in a form that respects scholarly standards and the political relevance of memory. Lacking responsible vision(s), the people, fed on rumours, platitudes, and clichés spread by the media and rabble-rousers of all kinds, absorb a repertoire of representations that sap their political imagination and historical consciousness rather than stimulate a desire for openness, reciprocity, and mutual recognition. This is how things stand now.

While there are exceptional successes in present-day Canada, there is also a dismal failure: there exists no overall representation of the country that recognizes what the Canadian historical experience has been, with all its insurmountable conflicts but also its undeniable force for recovery. This is the challenge – the challenge of (re)thinking the Canadian experience in its structural dissonances and fertile ambiguities – that I would like to take up in this short polemic, which should be seen as a highly exploratory, and rather risky, metahistorical essay. Essentially, I would like to reflect on Canadianness as a feature of the Canadian historical experience and a neglected, even forgotten theme of the great collective narrative of Canada.

It should be understood that my intention here is not to write a history of Canada from the perspective of Canadianness. That exercise would require a great deal of space and much more interpretive skill and wisdom than I possess. My intention, rather, is to examine, using the lens of Canadianness, how to represent the Canadian experience as a history of possibilities in a way that would be acceptable from the point of view of scholarly standards and political relevance as well as that of the ethics of remembering and social morality.

It goes without saying that such a process of interpretation implies that the narrator must clearly recognize the wounds, absurdities, errors, and irresponsibilities that have marked the country's history. The narrator would also have to show how Canada as a political entity has been formed out of the confrontation of conflicting conceptions and references concerning its nature and its future. But the narrator should also, out of consideration for his contemporaries' happiness and concern for the future, place himself in a position to build meaning, emphasizing the negotiation of constraints that has always inspired and fuelled the Canadian experience.

In many respects, this vision and this "practice" of Canada have for some time now been gradually eroding as the memory of the past and of the discernment of certain predecessors has become impoverished among the actors and decision-makers of the country.[4]

ON CANADIANNESS

Before going further, it is important that I define, if only briefly, what I mean by Canadianness. I will take care to avoid reducing Canadianness to the feeling of allegiance or belonging to the "nation" of Canada. I will also refrain from defining Canadianness as the "precipitate" of identity resulting from the formation of the state of Canada or the enterprise of Canadianization of the country. To me, Canadianness refers less to the legal reality of Canada or the current emblematic figure of the Canadian than to the *way of being together* that has developed within the space of social and political interrelations called Canada, at the heart of which Quebec has always been present.

For the sake of brevity, I will define Canadianness as the result of the empirical unfolding of the Canadian historical experience, and not as an intrinsic property of that experience – there is nothing in the country's past that reveals the presence of any Canadian "essence" that predisposes or overdetermines the actions of its inhabitants. In keeping with this logic, I will define Canadianness as a necessary condition for the ongoing relationships among communities that have lived in a situation of forced interdependence and manageable (in)difference within a space of proximity (eastern North America) that was quickly structured as the political space that became Canada, by competing powers that were dominating, prudent, and limited in their hegemonic claims.

The Canadian historical experience was, and still is, the expression of tensions and frictions between centripetal and centrifugal forces, sometimes working together and sometimes working against each other. It has also been an experience of going beyond these tensions and frictions through considered actions and trial and error to reach adjustments in order to go from one political situation to another. An interesting aspect of these adjustments, and one that is frustrating for many observers, is that although the adjustments are attempts to provide continuity with previous political situations, they have never solved the "Canadian equation," which has not just one common denominator but several joint denominators, including, unavoidably, Quebec. Although at first glance this situation seems disappointing and deplorable, it merits being looked at from a positive point of view since it has had consequences that, overall, were positive for Canada's development.

Historically, the absence of a solution to the Canadian equation has led to a kind of ambiguity of being for the people and the country, which has repeatedly proven fruitful for moving forward. By "ambiguity of being," I mean that the events that have been catalysts of Canadian development have generally led to ambivalence rather than univocity, to a certain open-endedness, variability, and flexibility of destiny. In other words, despite many attempts by minor and major actors and thinkers to bend Canadian destiny in a particular direction, it has never been possible to focus the development of the country according to a single structuring principle. Nor has it been possible to separate the future of the country from its past – to re-found Canada by ignoring the previous presences that have shaped it. Nor has it been possible to impose on the inhabitants of the country a single "practice" or a single vision of Canada, or to eliminate or ignore the will of the constituent communities of the country to assert themselves at any price, with and against other communities in the Canadian landscape. Thus, in practice, Canada has evolved, and continues to evolve, between the possibilities provided by its actors in seeking to overcome its constitutive dissonances and ambiguities – those resulting from its structural and structuring duality in particular – and the aporias resulting from all attempts to eliminate those dissonances and ambiguities through anthems to harmony and national unity.

Drawing on the metaphor of dissonance and the concept of ambiguity, Canadianness may be seen as the propensity to acknowledge:

- that conflict, tensions, and disagreements are at the heart of any relationship of forced interdependence among communities;
- that the clash of these contradictory dynamics gives rise to openings and possibilities for the future;
- that political activity must not, through lack of imagination, squander its energies in the administration of what is merely tolerable, but must attempt to broker outcomes that may seem impossible.

Defined in this way, Canadianness is the country's potential to regenerate itself by taking advantage of any inclination or obligation to reconcile the opposites that have been part of its historical development. Canadianness is this willingness on the part of Canada's historical actors to accept discord and to favour mediation – for reasons of political realism, inspired vision, or simply the desire to avert power struggles that could be counterproductive for the country's future. Canadianness is the recognition of positive possibilities for Canada's future in its dissonances and ambiguities. In my view, this aspect of Canadian history is the country's most remarkable characteristic, and its narrative remains largely unwritten.

HISTORICAL NARRATIVE AND MEMORY

Before getting to the meat of the subject, I would like to return to the quasi-postulate of my reflection, which I mentioned briefly at the beginning of this chapter. Is it acceptable, without neglecting the advantage of the scholar's position in any process involving knowledge, to reflect from an ethical point of view on the terms and conditions of the production of historical meaning in a collectivity? For that is the challenge posed by historical understanding in today's world: not only to restore what has been in all its complexity, but also, through the act of interpretation, to propose historical and narrative frameworks that will pave the way for the future. In the discipline of history, it may well be, as I have noted above, that hope, like critical vigilance, should be present at the start of the narrative.

The idea that the moral dimension is an intrinsic part of the act of interpretation is hardly astounding. It has long been an accepted principle that knowledge in the humanities and social sciences should culminate not in the complacent acceptance of facts as normality, but rather in the discovery of the means to critically go beyond those facts. Indeed, the social sciences are inextricably associated with humanistic reflection on human action. Without such reflection, which is a central dimension of political life as it is understood in the Western philosophical tradition, thought exists only as cold, utilitarian knowledge capable of serving any cause, even the cause of evil, and sanctioning or legitimizing it. As Hannah Arendt noted in an important article published in the early 1970s, the accumulation of knowledge can, paradoxically, inhibit us in relation to this duty to think that factual reality awakens, or should awaken, by virtue of its existence. For the brilliant Jewish intellectual, knowledge divorced from moral considerations is nothing less than an "inability to think."[5]

Several authors, following Paul Ricoeur,[6] have brought out how much the factuality of the past calls for a narration that breathes meaning into it in order to achieve historical self-realization and thus transcendence. Clearly, action demands narrative; or, in other words, narrative is the realization of action, a consubstantial element of its factuality. Moreover, there is no opposition, but rather a dialectical complementarity, between action and narrative.

Let me draw the consequences of this argument, which I have, obviously, simplified for my purposes: in the same way that action calls for narrative in order to realize itself, the past demands history in order to fulfill itself. Without the illumination provided by the discipline of history, by the narrative created through the human exercise of thought and the production of intelligibility from the factual raw material, the past is impotent, dormant, orphaned, and incomplete. It is incomplete because there is between the past and the present no opposition, but rather a mutual dependency of meaning in the consciousness of tomorrow. This idea of a consciousness of tomorrow and for tomorrow is of paramount importance. It makes us envision the relationship to ancestors as a duty not of memory but of custodianship, that is, of mediation by contemporaries with respect to descendants.

It is in this context of an intractable tension between action and narrative, knowledge and politics, the past and the future that the problem of the narrative of Canadian history must be seen. The challenge a narrator has to meet is not simply to produce a text that is accurate from the point of view of the complexity of the past and the winding paths the inhabitants of Canada have continually taken in confronting the contingencies of the country's evolution. That text also has to be politically relevant to the current form of a collectivity that is seeking to define itself according to a horizon to be opened up and built.

THE GREAT NATIONAL NARRATIVE IN CRISIS[7]

In recent years, many people throughout Canada have expressed their distress at the state of the great national collective narrative and its apparent inability to generate shared aspirations.[8] The most scathing criticism, which has come from historians who support a Canadian national approach, has been directed against pluralistic history, which has been blamed in the bluntest terms for conveying an empty identity that will weaken the national fibre and link the country's past to the contemporary squabbles of lobbies seeking political legitimacy.[9] By pluralistic history, I mean the narrative that recognizes the spatial, ethnic, social, cultural, and gender factors in the making of the country. It is a narrative that tends to present an image of Canada "from below" (focusing on the diversity of experience of the inhabitants) rather than "from above" (emphasizing the great processes of establishing the "nation" as an aggregate entity). According to this narrative, the "country" appears as the sum of its many parts and its particularistic visions, and not as the expression of a homogeneous whole covering its parts with a single aura of identity.

Pluralistic history has experienced a meteoric rise in Canada since the beginning of the 1970s,[10] and has become part of the general rise of cultural and social "minorities" of all kinds and the public expression of individual belonging and allegiances – while at the same time conferring recognition on this trend. It must be acknowledged that although pluralistic history cannot be reduced to the replacement of the "old" parameters of Canadian identity, such as cultural-linguistic duality, with new parameters, in particular civic patriotism, democratic individualism, and multiculturalism,[11] it has never been dissociated from that eminently political enterprise. Generally, pluralistic history has fuelled and been fuelled by what has been called the perspective of "limited identities," a view of the country based on the recognition and promotion of diversity as the cardinal virtue of the Canadian historical experience.

There is no doubt that pluralistic history, which has marked historiographic production in French Quebec as well as English Canada, has resulted in an extraordinary enrichment and increase in complexity of the representations of the country's past. In this, there is no going back. The "renationalization" of Canadian history desired by certain thinkers who are nostalgic for the old visions and interpretations of the country seems inadequate, even inappropriate, historically and politically, in the context of the current hegemony of the discourse of diversity and the advances of pluralistic history.[12] This being said, there are two reasonable criticisms that can be made of pluralistic history and that its proponents have not yet answered convincingly.[13]

The first criticism concerns this history's lack of perspective and its practitioners' lack of explicit concern for the ordering and ranking of the dynamics, forces, and factors they highlight in Canada's past. Of course, no one will dispute that Canada was built on the diversity of its parts. It is also necessary to distinguish, in the array of "limited identities" found in the past of the country, those that have had a central, structural impact on its development. While doing national history is an enterprise that remains totally relevant in this new century, if only because the nation-state, even in the context of globalization and local or regional restructuring of the world, is still for most people the main reference, the meaningful place, and the major, even the essential horizon of their existence, we must be very aware of the challenge inherent in this kind of history, the challenge of forging an appropriate framework to relate what made the country yesterday and what constitutes it today.[14]

The second criticism, which follows from the first one, is metahistorical. It concerns the meaning of the Canadian historical experience. It might be claimed that the only acceptable truth in the interpretation of Canada's past is one that emphasizes the multiplicity of points of view, and thus of "specific truths." However, it seems inappropriate for an interpreter to leave the past in such a state of conceptual indeterminacy, which expresses, legitimizes, and leads to nothing but political impotence.[15] The role of the intellectual in general, and the historian in particular, is to reintroduce into the raw material of the past a meaning that will be useful in the building of the future. Without this production of meaning, the past and the present are in danger of getting bogged down in empirical confusion. Like life itself, the past needs to be gathered into a narrative unit in order to be rid of its evasive, dispersed quality. It is in this respect that the pluralistic narrative – which presents Canada's past in terms of particularistic visions, thematic vignettes, and disconnected scenes – fails to provide an overall representation of the country that is productive and responsible.[16] It fails in its function because, instead of acknowledging Canada's constitutive differences and capitalizing on them to relaunch the country's future, it treats them as equivalent or is incapable of going beyond them in an original overview of the Canadian experience.[17]

In practice, pluralistic history subjects the material of the past to a false scholarly correctness and an insipid philosophy of knowledge, that of non-differentiation as the principle of historical objectivity and narrativization of the past.[18] Hence the history of Canada appears equivalent to the sum of what can be discovered and told about the country's past. To the proponents of pluralistic history, the ideal historical narrative of Canada would include and express all points of view of the country. This model narrative would, by the scope of its coverage, fill in the gaps through which other narratives that are considered more "biased" and less rich could find a way in. Given such a desire for histori(ographi)cal "perfection" (or such intolerance?), it is understandable that it is difficult to achieve any comprehensive synthesis of the Canadian experience.

From the perspective of pluralistic history, Canada no longer exists as a normative, teleological, or transcendent category – which is certainly a correct position – but rather as the accidental "precipitate" of the multiplicity of human actions carried out in the space designated by that name. In many respects this is an inadequate and finally unsatisfactory interpretive position, since it leads to a loss of shared aspirations, a watering down of the meaning of the country, and an impasse in terms of its overall representations, which precisely translates the political impotence I spoke of above. At present, the consequences of this political impotence, which are felt sharply in Quebec, seem particularly evident with respect to the integration of that "province" into the Canadian framework.

What is to be done under the circumstances? Should we accept this interpretive impasse and this political impotence or should we attempt together to go beyond it? If we opt to go beyond it, how do we connect and combine what constitutes the substance of the country (the "limited identities") in the form of a dynamic, characteristic whole (Canada)? Is it even possible to envision a narrative, historical mediation of this political dilemma? If so, what meaning should be given to the Canadian historical experience so as to convey it in its irreducible dissonances and ambiguities and give it a momentum that will prevent it from getting trapped in the undertow of its constitutive frictions? In short, what narrative of Canada's past could be proposed that would hold the promise of a reunited country?

ON THE DIFFICULTY OF WRITING THE HISTORY OF CANADA'S PAST

To me it is clear that there is no future in a unitarist narrative that postulates a convergence of the structuring differences of Canada or calls for their sublimation in order to bring (back) to life a country that is sure of itself and affirms its identity.[19] Such a narrative has no future because it does not relate to the record of the lived past of the country now, nor did it ever. To suggest, as Jack Granatstein does, for example, that there are not several, not even two, histories of Canada, but only one great national saga inspired by a single unifying force, in which diversity melts into the unity of a positive common destiny to be resuscitated and celebrated, is, however "reconciliatory" and dithyrambic a vision, pure fabulation.[20] Similarly, to expunge from the conception of Canada the structuring dissension of the country, and thus to stretch the idea of the nation or the national political community until it is nothing more than an abstract ideal with no material basis, and to privilege only a single image of the country as renewed, progressive, bilingual, multicultural, civic, and post-modern – it is now abundantly clear that this offers no useful option.[21]

One of the "tragedies" of Canada – if I may call it that – involves the obsession, which is recurrent in the country's intellectual and political history, with doing something with Canada's past and present that cannot be rigorously supported by either that past or that present. And the hesitation, indeed the refusal, to acknowledge the central fact of the country is astonishing. It is as if that fact were embarrassing, as if there were a deviation, something fundamentally disturbing, in the Canadian historical experience. Surprisingly, this "pimple on the country's face" is the diversity that is characteristic of Canada, in particular the irreducible constitutive and structural duality of the Canadian collectivity, which the country has yet to go beyond.[22]

For a long time, the reservations concerning diversity and difference were related to the desire of Canadians of Anglo-Celtic origin to make Canada an anglophone country and state based on the British tradition[23] – but a state and country, to the displeasure of many, with a "minority" too numerous, concentrated, and strategically significant to be completely assimilated culturally or marginalized politically.[24] Hence the recognition granted to this "minority" – the French Canadians – which, through a process of self-affirmation that has gone on since the Cession of 1763, succeeded in establishing itself as one of the major political communities within the federation,[25] and did so despite the temporary suspension and even the partial reorientation of its quest for affirmation following the failed rebellions of 1837–38.

At the present time, the reservations shown by anglophone Canada concerning diversity and difference are based mostly on a fear of seeing the country fall completely into the American orbit. Full acceptance of the structural diversity and dissonance among regions and provinces and between the two major linguistic-cultural communities would, in the eyes of the majority of anglophone Canadians, weaken the nation. It would also force many decision-makers to admit that the multicultural representation of Canada, which competes symbolically and politically with the dualist representation,[26] promotes a folkloric view of the diversity of Canada, a view that is fuelled by the action of many ethnic pressure groups.[27] Acknowledging the existence of two great linguistic-cultural crucibles and recognizing their structuring effects on Canada's development would mean finally getting away from the perception of (French) Quebec in terms of infantilism and irresponsibility, incompetence and backwardness, a perception that is outdated but still operative within the federation.[28]

Major stakes are involved in a historical narrative of Canada that would recognize what the country has essentially been, structurally, for quite some time already – a narrative, in my view, of power relationships that have been more or less tense and unequal, made up of negotiated or imposed compromises and forced, unstable accommodations among regions and provinces and between the two main linguistic-cultural communities.[29] This is because envisaging Canada's past from the perspective of national unity or convergence of its "parts" is largely an artificial enterprise. But it is also because restoring Canada's past by focusing indiscriminately and uncritically on all the forces, factors, and dynamics whose interaction has built the country is no more valid an option. If the perspective of the highest common denominator (a country of confluences) proves unsatisfactory for Canada, that of the lowest or the multiple common denominator (Canada as a juxtaposition of "minorities") is no better. It is important to find a level of factual and narrative histori(ographi)cal articulation that makes it possible to conceptualize and represent Canada in its dissonant fabric, its unstable equilibrium, its distant proximities, and its stormy interdependencies – but that is difficult. We should be aware, however, that doing so would involve nothing less than a renewal of the most fertile and promising dimension of the Canadian historical experience, that of Canadianness, in order to build the future.

In this regard, the efforts of more than thirty years now toward a history of "limited identities" have opened up the factual space of Canadian history, making possible the "discovery" of a body of material from the past that did not immediately or readily belong to the history of Canada as a totalizing representation of the country. However, studies carried out from the perspective of "limited identities" have not, at least to date, provided a metahistorical narrative structure in the form of a comprehensive synthesis of the Canadian experience.[30]

Either this challenge was refused on the pretext that there could be no single integrated narrative of Canada or great efforts were made to present the country's history as that of a mosaic of peoples, ethnic groups, and social movements – with spatial, gender, or socio-economic ties – maintaining relationships of co-operation and antagonism or adapting, for better or worse, to their differences.[31] At any rate, no one has been able or willing to recognize explicitly any connecting framework that would distinguish, rank, order, and structure the elements that have gone into the "composition" of the Canadian historical experience. Rather than take up the difficult challenge of developing such a framework, which obviously gives rise to certain choices with respect to the premises of the narrative and of memory, historians "solved" the problem by telling the history of Canadians rather than that of Canada.[32]

Writing the history of the country from the perspective of its inhabitants, emphasizing the multiplicity of their practices and the diversity of their identities, has thus become an alternative to, even a panacea for, the challenge of organizing the factual material of Canada around a metahistorical conception of the Canadian experience. Presenting Canada as a land of immigrants and defining those immigrants accordingly, along with the Native peoples (the first inhabitants of Canada, or even the first Canadians), as the builders of the country has emerged in the context of pluralist discourse and narrative as a way of re-examining and reshaping Canada's past from a perspective that would be appropriate in terms of the country's diversity as well as the need to renew shared aspirations for the nation.[33] This kind of vision, which, on the one hand, balances and "squares" the driving forces of the country while avoiding distinguishing among them or ranking them according to the structuring effects of their actions, and, on the other hand, justifies the revision of the material of the past in terms of questions rooted primarily in the present, is not without problems. I will limit myself to discussing the fashionable representation of Canada as a land of immigrants structured mainly by the existence of a multiplicity of cultures.

It is certainly not false to present Canada as a country of immigrants. It is also important to recognize that, by virtue of their numbers and their predominance in the space which became Canada, these immigrants, who initially came from relatively homogeneous population pools (France and the British Isles), constituted the original cultural poles to which newcomers from throughout Europe gravitated and, over generations, conformed. It will readily be acknowledged that immigrants of the "second wave," most of them from origins other than French or British, have intensely coloured the Frenchness or Englishness they finally adopted when they settled in the country. The political culture of the inhabitants of the provinces of Manitoba, Saskatchewan, and Alberta, where many immigrants from Eastern Europe settled at the turn of the 20th century, is a good example of this. It would be wrong, however, to think that the force of attraction or the power of assimilation of the two majority cultures established in the country was countered by the arrival and development of people of other ethnic origins. Rather, these people in the long term integrated voluntarily, as a result of pressure or the lack of other options, into the dominant cultures, which they both reinforced and refined.

This was the situation until the 1960s. The broadening of the sources of immigration to Canada gave rise to a more complex collectivity, but it did not change the structure of the country. Canada continued to have two effective "majorities," anglophone and francophone, and this has actually been reinforced by the fact that, despite its multiculturalism, it recognizes two official languages, English and French.

Of course, there are citizens of widely varied ethnic origins who have more or less powerful organizations to promote their interests in the political arena and the public sphere. Nonetheless, Canada, nearly a hundred and forty years after its creation, is still structured along a line of tension of which the poles of attraction and repulsion are the anglophone and francophone communities.[34] There is no significant social or political movement in Canada that has not been marked by this duality, which many people would like to eliminate, diminish, or ignore, but which seems ineradicable. Like it or not, in spite of the existence of "global forces" that cut across the country, it is still necessary, to achieve anything civically, politically, and socially in Canada, to be integrated into the anglophone or the francophone "majority." Insofar as these "majorities" are redefining the horizon of their identities, they provide both an incomparable force of attraction and a certain constancy in the empirical space of cultural transactions. The pressure on newcomers to integrate is particularly strong in the case of children, who assimilate on a large scale, especially linguistically and culturally – which does not mean that, in private or within small enduring communities, they do not practise their ancestral cultures in more or less syncretic, even hybrid, forms. Throughout Canada, Americanness, experienced in English or in French, is a powerful factor of "de-ethnicization" of immigrants and "reacculturation" of their descendants toward an identity profile structurally marked and fed by Frenchness or Englishness[35] – so much so that, in spite of everything that is said, recent immigration to Canada has not significantly altered the structural duality of the country. It has simply provided it with a new basis that is broader and more complex. While the concept of "founding peoples" has fallen into disuse in the repertoire of overall representations of the country, those of anglophone and francophone Canadians, which are much broader than the those of French Canadians and English Canadians, have lost none of their relevance for describing and expressing Canada. In this context, articulating the Canadian experience in a narrative framework that stresses the constitutive duality of the country is certainly not going out on a limb in relation to the current situation in Canada. In fact, the current situation represents more of a continuation of the past than a rupture with it.[36]

The Native peoples are a special case. In total, depending on what criterion is used – legal status, cultural origin, or ancestry – they currently make up between 2.7 and 4.3 per cent of the Canadian population.[37] At the time of the first sustained contact with Europeans in the mid-sixteenth century, there were approximately 40,000 Aboriginal people living in what is today Quebec, and perhaps half a million in Canada. The Amerindians were decimated by diseases resulting from the arrival of the Europeans, diseases that spread with the increasing physical presence of the new "invaders." There is no doubt that the contribution of the Native peoples was vital to the Europeans' survival and success on "Canadian soil." Similarly, the non-Native cultures over time assimilated techniques, models, concepts, expressions, symbolic representations, and beliefs belonging to the Native cultures – to such an extent that many researchers have no hesitation in identifying the origins of many facets of contemporary Canada in those Native cultures.[38]

That observation is justified; from the beginning, aboriginality proved to be a central dimension of emerging Canadianness. By this I mean that the first contacts between non-Native and Native peoples revealed the possibility of transactions that would be advantageous for both parties, and even alliances that would be beneficial for the prosperity of both.[39] It is often said that New France was able to survive in the context of the French-English rivalry in America only through an exceptional network of Indian alliances.[40] Of course, this situation of self-interested co-operation in no way meant that there were not intercultural disagreements or conflicts. This being said, the real "country" was being built empirically around a duality that, while not ideal, nevertheless gave rise to accommodations between sovereign communities living in forced interdependence.

Subsequent history would largely destroy this initial capital of reciprocity. As a colonial enterprise and as a "modern" state and political project, Canada developed despite the presence of the Native communities (or over them), leaving them to rot in reserves, those institutionalized parentheses of its development, abandoning them to the eternity of winter cold, or appropriating their ancestral lands by fair means or force of law. Thus it is inaccurate to claim that the Native peoples were at the origin of the founding of Canada. On the contrary, the history of the formation of Canada, including the pre-Confederation period, is one of reduction of the Native peoples to a state of dependency and their progressive marginalization as the original occupants of the "Canadian" territory. It was also an enterprise of systematic denial of the Native contribution to the development of Canada.[41]

One could, out of political correctness or to make honourable amends, reconsider previous actions and decide now to view the Native peoples as "founding peoples" or the "first nations" of Canada, even to make them the symbolic ancestors of the nation of "All we Canadians." To do so would be to alter the meaning of the past. To define the Native peoples as "pre-Canadians" is a misapprehension of history. It is an interpretive about-turn inspired by major political stakes, which themselves are dictated by the search for an easy solution to the integration of the Native peoples.[42] In any case, it is a false mediation. The challenge lies elsewhere – in reinscribing aboriginality as a structural dimension of Canadianness, in other words, putting the Native presence and identity back at the heart of the political dynamics of the country.[43]

Contrary to what may at first seem to be the case, the two views are quite different. The first view (the Native peoples as "founding peoples" and "ancestors of the nation") originates in a desire to alter the meaning of the past for the sake of the immediate imperatives of the consensual, harmonious building of a future freed of the burden of history and its wounds. The path chosen is to correct the past, to heal the wounds so that they will eventually disappear. The second view (aboriginality as a structural dimension of Canadianness) arises from a decision to leave the wound open in order to regenerate the bruised body. It means recognizing the existence of the wound so as to transform it into possibilities for the future.

This idea of the transformation of wounds into possibilities – a transformation brought about through the narration of an interpreter seeking to rediscover the lost spirit and practice of Canadianness – is interesting. This may perhaps be a new horizon that could orient those who want to rethink and rewrite the history of Canada.

THE CANADIAN EXPERIENCE AS A HISTORY OF POSSIBILITIES

I will begin with two postulates to which I ascribe no universal significance or value but that I consider valid in the specific case of the Canadian historical experience:

1 It is not necessary to repudiate or forget Canada's past in order to be able, as Canadians, Quebecers, and Native peoples, to live and develop together.[44]
2 To contribute to the eventual fulfillment of this destiny, it nevertheless seems appropriate to transform memory into a regenerative consciousness through the production of a narrative of recognition, mourning, and hope.

In this context, the question that seems pertinent, historiographically as well as politically, is the following: can we find in the Canadian historical experience – which absolutely cannot be reduced to the single political process of the establishment of the federation and the formation of the central state – the material, the factuality through which it would be possible to move beyond the limitations and sometimes the aporias of current representations of the country? It is certainly possible to answer this question in the affirmative. In fact, just as modernity contains within itself its own critical principles, Canada's historical experience contains within it the potential to go beyond itself.

This does not of course mean that the Canadian historical experience should be presented as a great victory of common reason and collective progress over special interests and the forces of regression. It would be wrong to substitute for the lucid narration of the past a narrative that would be nothing but a pure ideological enterprise or an attempt to reinvent tradition. The practice of history must always in every respect be marked by rigour.

At the same time, the narrator cannot avoid the obligation to give the past a chance to express itself in all its complexity and ambivalence. Like the leader of the chorus in Greek drama, who gave voice to the fears and questions within the actors so that they could, with the audience, overcome the tragic situation and go on to other things, the interpreter is the one who gives words to the hidden, ignored, or neglected meaning of what has been in order to enable those he is addressing to go beyond what seemed or still seems impassable. It is the duty of the historian to recall and reveal to his or her contemporaries the potential for mediation and regeneration contained in the past so as to enable the present to rise above what it is and go beyond its impasses. In the case of Canada, the potential for regeneration and the ability to go beyond the country's impasses is what I associate with Canadianness, the history of which, unthought, forgotten, usurped, or trampled on, is not, for all that, unthinkable, irretrievable, or irreparable. I will state my views on this question in greater detail.

By a history of Canadianness I mean that narrative in which the explicit, irreducible diversity of society and identities in Canada – class and gender identities, local and urban identities, ethnic and minority identities of all kinds – fuses to form meaningful realities and contexts of incorporation, organization, reference, and expression of powers, such as, for the period from the mid-nineteenth century to today at least, the large historical regions of the country, the provinces, and the major linguistic-cultural communities discussed above. Of course, there is no question here of circumscribing the basic vitality of lifeworlds and multiple identifications in categories that would overshadow the empirical experience of action. The exercise implies, rather, recognizing that what takes place on a small scale at the level of practices should be linked to certain structural realities that determine, inspire, or sanction the local phenomena and the multiplicity of individual and collective initiatives. Among these structural realities, the focus and the backbone of the history of Canada, are linguistic-cultural dualism, regionalism, and provincialism, which is closely associated with regionalism.[45] These structural realities, which are related to the existence of established powers that accommodate those famous "limited identities," cannot be ignored or dismissed as secondary, or we risk losing sight of the meaning of the Canadian historical experience. That is how important and central they are to any narrative of the country.

By a history of Canadianness I mean a narrative that is built on something other than a sterile historical correctness in which the interpretive quest is confused with the current imperatives of a policy of wholesale recognition of communities competing in the public arena and the space of collective representations. Historical narration should never take the form of retrospective identity politics. History is not a matter of equity, but of rigour. We cannot subordinate the past to the present.

By a history of Canadianness I mean, finally, that the scholarly spirit takes responsibility for itself in a lucid, realistic narrative of the past, a narrative in which the heritage is conveyed with a duty to the future, a narrative in which the interpreter follows the movement of the past, avoids betraying its meaning, and seeks, using subtle, precise language, to describe the complexity and multidimensionality of what has been and to relieve it of its harmfulness (wounds) and exploit its accumulated capital of goodness (possibilities).

The Canadian experience as a history of possibilities is the material the concept of Canadianness allows us to discover and the horizon that concept enables us to revive. To accept Canadianness as the structuring and structural matrix of the Canadian experience would, in my view, be to adopt the perspective of two majorities living side by side and maintaining conflictual relations within the framework of a colonial society, at first, and a liberal society, later, without allowing themselves to be subordinated in a political community of convergence (the ideal of a unitary Canada that subsumes the discord of its parts) or involved in some disembodied civic project rushing toward a rootless future (the Canada of the *Charter of Rights and Freedoms*).

To accept Canadianness as the structuring and structural matrix of the Canadian experience would also be to see how Canada's past, while undeniably the theatre of power relationships that have often been resolved in unfortunate ways (which I describe as wounds), has at the same time been, unceasingly, a place of dialogue among actors seeking to assert themselves without denying their quest (I am speaking here of possibilities). To illustrate my point, let us look at one example, a significant one: it is in the political space created by the perpetual tension between the desire of the English powers to marginalize the French fact in early America and in Canada (wound) and the need to dialogue with the francophones so as to deal with their desire to endure and develop (possibility) that the francophones, from their seat in Quebec, became a major political community in Canada.[46] Similar dynamics prevailed between the powers of central Canada and those of eastern and western Canada, with the former seeking to impose their hegemony over the entire Canadian economic space from the Montreal-Toronto-Ottawa triangle and the latter resisting this "hinterlandization" that aimed to subordinate them to metropolitan interests. There is no doubt that envisaging a narrative for Canada's future requires that we acknowledge this axial process, this dialectic of wounds and possibilities in the country's historical evolution.

Developing a narrative for Canada's future also implies that we must be able to approach the question of the relationship with Native peoples in the country. In my view, as I have said, they are not among the "founding communities" of Canada.[47] They were simply there, having lived in the territory of the "country" for a long time and appropriated the space in their own way. Naturally they were still there when the British North America Act was enacted. While they were not passive in the face of what was happening in their environment, but rather sought to protect their interests through alliances, it was very difficult, even impossible, for them to react as masters of their destiny to the global change that marked the Atlantic world in the sixteenth, seventeenth, and eighteenth centuries, a world into which America was becoming increasingly integrated.

Given that they were effectively left out of the British colonial project after 1763 – a "banishment" that was renewed with respect to the "Canadian project" in 1867 – it seems strange to now try to reintegrate the Native peoples into the Canadian framework as "founding peoples" or the "first nations" *of the country.* These are contrived designations, whose meaning is to be found in the dilemmas of the present rather than the reality of the past. In fact, precisely for reasons related to that past, it seems incongruous for the Native peoples to demand any rights by invoking the artificial meta-identities assigned or willingly granted to them by the non-Native peoples.[48] It is, however, possible for them to demand reparation for their reduction over the centuries: their dispossession of territory, first of all, then gradually of political activity, then of all the attributes of the modern world.[49] They are also entitled to demand special recognition on the basis of the decisive effect of their presence on the success of the European "graft" in the St Lawrence Valley – a graft that eventually gave rise to the establishment of a political entity, Canada, whose presence and enduring influence the Native peoples must take into account in any vision of their future.

Politically, the idea of self-government, with the reasonable prerogatives and limits this form of sovereignty-association entails – which would re-establish a certain tradition of alliances between Amerindians and Europeans that existed in the seventeenth and eighteenth centuries – seems promising, at least for Native peoples living outside urban centres.[50] Histori(ographi)cally, any narrative must give prominence to the long process of reduction and dispossession that has marked the situation of the Native peoples.

Of course, in view of recent developments in ethnohistory, it is also important to emphasize the cultural transfers that have characterized relationships between Native and non-Native peoples through the ages, particularly during the pre-Confederation period.[51] But the existence of these cultural transfers should not make us lose sight of the key fact that from the beginning of the nineteenth century the Native peoples have played a marginal role in the structuring and development of the world they both belong to and at the same time are rejected from. While it is true that Canada would not have been what it was and is without the initial presence of the Native peoples – who have never lost or given up their consciousness of their inalienable cultural specificity – it would be going too far to suggest that the "Native factor" in the final analysis had a preponderant weight on the "Canadian scale." The roles of actors and factors in history cannot be altered with impunity.

It thus seems very difficult to write the history of Canada on the basis of the Native "factor" or "element" without reducing the Canadian experience to only one of its dimensions or elevating the Native peoples to the rank of dominant actors in the country's evolution. However, the opposite is possible: writing a (Canadian) history of the Native peoples that would have as a key dimension the invasive, destructive, and alienating "factors" of the non-Natives and the establishment of the country.[52] This was the task the Royal Commission on Aboriginal Peoples took on, primarily if not exclusively.[53] Perhaps paradoxically, the possibility for a histori(ographi)cally and politically acceptable reintegration of the Native peoples into the Canadian framework (but not into the emblematic image of the country) lies in the recognition of the wound inflicted upon them – this recognition being precisely an openness to dialogue, a readiness to rediscover a forgotten or lost aspect of Canadianness, to envision the possibility of a future of honourable tension, mutual respect, and equal recognition of participants in the country that is to be recovered.

There remains the regional dimension of the Canadian experience to be taken into consideration, from the perspective of a possible rewriting of the history of Canada that would be accurate in terms of facts and, to come back to Arendt, acceptable in terms of the obligation to think about political life. Regionalism, which ties in with and influences provincial reality and even urban reality much more than it counters them, is a structural and structuring dimension of the country's evolution. Over time, regionalism has come to occupy a place in the overall vision and practice of Canada that is just as important, perhaps more important in some respects, than the linguistic-cultural duality of the country. Regionalism also accelerated the transition of the Confederation of Canada to federated Canada, the seeds of which were certainly contained in the terms of Confederation but for which the effective conditions might not have existed – but this is a very different issue from that of nation building. Writing the history of Canada from a regionalist perspective does not mean betraying the country's past. It means recognizing that Canada was initially built, and continues to exist, in the irreducible tension between a central state with unitarist claims and potential, on the one hand, and a variety of mechanisms operating at the level of regions or provinces, on the other hand. From this point of view, Quebec seems to be in a unique situation since it is the only space in Canada to hold the triple status of province, historical region, and principal seat of one of the country's two major linguistic-cultural groups.

According to the view I am expressing here, Canada is not the fulfillment of unity in diversity.[54] It is the irreducible expression of an asymmetrical tension between centripetal and centrifugal forces. This tension (or dissonance) is the very place of the expression and condensation of the wounds and possibilities that have always been the raw material of the Canadian experience. To want to escape from this dialectic of wounds and possibilities, to want to rewrite the history of Canada while steering clear of this creative as well as destructive tension on which the country's history was built, means, once again, to lose the meaning of Canadianness.

Of course, this view is not shared by all the actors and interpreters who, in the past or present, have reflected on the Canadian experience. That is hardly surprising. We know what a proliferation there has been in the past, and still today, of decision-makers and thinkers who have sought to end this tension, which they have seen as a problem rather than a source of inventiveness and regeneration of the Canadian experience. Until now, perhaps fortunately, all their initiatives have failed. It is possible to assert that Canada was forged historically through a set of lost wagers by dominant powers and majorities guided by intransigent reason against individuals and minorities determined to endure over time, constantly asserting themselves and seeking to deal with the reality of things and peoples instead of rejecting this reality or exiling themselves in narrow places of being.

Writing the history of this insistence on self-assertion and endurance – an approach that requires the interpreter to go to the heart of a dialectic of resistances and offensives among the communities involved, and thus of the asymmetrical accommodations among them – means finding ways to recognize the potential for recovery inherent in the Canadian experience. It means facing head-on the operation of transforming wounds into possibilities. It means returning to the idea of mourning, which, as we have seen, is neither discharge nor renunciation with respect to what has been, but rather the production of surplus value of meaning, for life and for the future.

RECOVERING THE MEANING OF THE CANADIAN EXPERIENCE

What am I to conclude at the end of this essay in metahistory?

My first observation concerns the limits of pluralistic history. While the extraordinary broadening that has occurred in the production of historical writing on Canada's past has undeniably led to the proliferation of our representations of the country, it must be admitted that, in this scholarly movement that also follows the mood of the time, we have lost the meaning of the Canadian historical experience. One may wonder whether, all in all, the Canadian collectivity has come out the winner in this exchange between scholarship and politics. In any case, the question deserves to be asked realistically. Historical narrative cannot be written outside of all moral, ethical, and political considerations. It must involve the search for an optimal narrative position between the factuality and irreducible complexity of the past, on the one hand, and, on the other hand, the need to arrive at interpretive syntheses that give meaning to those who, in order to build the future, need to place themselves in a relationship of recognition and distance with their predecessors and with what has been.

My second observation concerns the need, in order to describe Canada's historical experience in all its constitutive ambiguities, to use formulations that successfully bring out this ambiguity rather than hide or attenuate it. To my mind, there is nothing paradoxical or contradictory in this ambiguity. On the contrary, it seems to me to hold the promise of a fruitful dialectic between wounds and possibilities, refusal to communicate and dialogue. From my point of view, the ambiguity of the Canadian historical experience is not a manifestation of a "national failure" or a regrettable digression from a destiny related to the ideal type of the nation-state. Nor is it the expression of an inability to be and to live together on the part of the country's inhabitants. It is an original path that must be recognized as such, a trajectory whose resources must be exploited to fuel the future.

To me, it thus seems appropriate to use disconcerting concepts such as "unstable equilibrium," "distant proximities," "dissonant fabric," "stormy interdependencies" to describe the Canadian historical experience. To represent Canada in the constant movement of its order or disorder (whichever one prefers), let us imagine a Calder mobile whose elements, continually balancing with or against each other, produce a kind of dissonant composition of real and virtual motifs in which harmony is always "under construction," never achieved and continually being recreated.

In any case, the challenge for the next generation of historians who want to (re)think Canada is not to conceal the past for the sake of the future nor to magnify that past to save the country from the apprehended future. The challenge is perhaps more to acknowledge what the past was, including its "dark sides," and, in full awareness, to free themselves, through a narrative marked by recognition and distance, from what seems inappropriate for heirs to carry into the future.

Articulating the recognition and hope at the heart of the interpretive act under the aegis of the two cardinal virtues of critical vigilance and moral judgment is the ideal manifestation of the objectivity that, beyond any other consideration, must be expressed in the narrator's capacity to think the human experience in all its tensions and its power of transcendence, that is, in its abiding humanity. Because, as Pascal said, to think is to move on.

CHAPTER FOUR

The Fate of the Past: Risks and Challenges of Turning the Past into Narrative

(Notes on Jacques Godbout's The Fate of America*)*

Jacques Godbout, an important and controversial figure in the Quebec intellectual landscape of the past forty years, has always been an iconoclast, and has created his public persona and his iconic depictions of history in paradoxical, ambiguous, and ambivalent terms. An author and filmmaker, Godbout has produced an important body of work, including novels, non-fiction, poetry, newspaper articles, and fictional and documentary films.[1]

One of Godbout's documentaries, entitled in English *The Fate of America,* was made in 1996, one year after the last referendum on sovereignty in Quebec. It is of particular interest to me because of my concern with memory and collective narrative.[2] In this ninety-minute production, which he himself calls "an impertinent film, a documentary comedy that mixes fiction and reality,"[3] Godbout undertakes to get to the heart of the pivotal event of the great collective narrative of Quebecers, the event that turned their world upside down: the Battle of the Plains of Abraham, on 13 September 1759, in which the British defeated the French. Godbout is trying to understand the precise impact and meaning of that battle in the history, memory, imaginary, and identity of the Canadiens, who later became French Canadians, and then Quebecers.

Given that after so many years the Battle of the Plains of Abraham continues to arouse bitterness, and even, for some people – including his own father – to fuel a muted or impassioned resentment of "the English," Godbout wonders if it is time to move on to a narrative and interpretative regime that would free the event from the ghosts of the past. But in that case, he asks, what kind of history of the Battle of the Plains of Abraham would free contemporary Quebecers from this burden of memory without "sanitizing" them as historical beings rooted in a culture or condemning them to amnesia?

IN SEARCH OF A HISTORY

To take on the difficult task of unravelling the historical aftermath of the Battle of the Plains of Abraham – and with it, perhaps, the destiny of francophone Quebecers in America! – Godbout teams up with two associates, a pair of opposite types who complement each other, whom he uses both as references and foils in constructing a new historical narrative of the event, a narrative intended to be liberating for the historical consciousness of Quebecers of French-Canadian heritage. The first associate, a cameraman and Godbout's assistant, is Philippe Falardeau.[4] With a guileless approach to life and the apparent belief that the past has the right of veto over his material and its uses, Falardeau plays a kind of "straight man," the embodiment of honesty and earnestness. As a well-trained documentary filmmaker, he repeats to anyone who will listen, especially his boss and mentor, Godbout, that the past cannot be manipulated with impunity, that the narration of the past must obey certain established rules, and that it would be appropriate to consult historians, the vestal virgins of true knowledge against the proponents of common sense and popular wisdom, in order to have an accurate idea of the past.

Godbout's second partner, whom he meets in London, where he too is working on a screenplay about the famous battle of 1759 – but for some Hollywood producers – is René-Daniel Dubois.[5] Dubois, who has "real-life" experience and an awareness that things are given meaning only by being articulated in words, plays the role of a kind of trickster in relation to Godbout, a two-faced consciousness that is also attractive, even salutary in many respects. Trained in the school of fiction, Dubois defends a view that is basically quite simple, but remarkably strong: the past is unthinkable without a plot; the plot curbs the unbearable lightness of being and the fluidity of life; history is essentially the story of the past, in the sense that actors always make a (hi)story out of what the past has made of them. In other words, fiction is the insatiable mistress of man and it is illusory to try to separate them; talking about the past necessarily involves a narrative mediation in which the clarity and coherence of the account inevitably (will) win out over the chaos of facts and the paradoxical complexity of things; in the end, there is nothing to understand of the past except what is said of it and deduced from it after the fact.

It is precisely the orientation of this *ex post* narrative that poses a problem – particularly for Godbout, who is still hesitating between the models proposed by his colleagues, that of a serious, credible historical account and that of an extravagant narrative of what has been.

TWO NARRATIVE MODELS

As a novice documentary filmmaker, Falardeau wants to construct the best possible narrative and interpretation of the Battle of the Plains of Abraham and its aftermath, respecting the established approach, that is, marshalling the facts, basing himself on solid ground rather than on discourse, taking the context into account, looking at things from a number of angles, complexifying the investigation so as to establish links, the goal being to understand, explain, and provide answers, and to abandon fantasy and fiction, even if this entails acknowledging certain shadowy areas or elements that resist any overall interpretation, but without ever abdicating the narrator's ultimate challenge to reach a point of view of the past that is well founded, nuanced, and informed.

Dubois, on the other hand, as a scriptwriter who must immediately and inescapably confront the constraints of meaning, whatever the cost, has to resolve any problem that jeopardizes the possibility of a clear, unequivocal interpretation. He must leave nothing to chance. He has to conceal the gaps and unravel the paradoxes. He has to fabricate coherence and continuity in order to create intelligibility. His logic is obvious: no intelligibility, no communication, therefore nothing to recount. No history, no heir; no heir, no future; nothing but the present, a succession of events with no connections. This sounds risky, and rather boring, and Dubois opts for a bold approach and a definitive history as opposed to a many-voiced narrative and limited interpretation.

ONE TAKES FLIGHT, THE OTHERS STAY ON THE GROUND

At the end of Godbout's film narrative – which records his and Dubois's trials and tribulations – we learn that Dubois has managed to write a screenplay wrapping up the past in a beautiful linear story with heroes and villains, saints and whores, solemnity and modesty, courage and fear, flags and loves, good guys and bad guys. Beaming with contentment, his manuscript under his arm, he flies off to Hollywood certain that 1759 will indeed have its story, which will become a history, and perhaps even History – with a Hollywood flavour of course – the history the public expects and that will galvanize the audience.

Falardeau and Godbout, apparently unable to untangle the knots of the past and create an objectively acceptable narrative of the events of 1759, are left feeling rather sheepish, with no script, no story to tell, and no audience to tell it to. Envious and resentful, like two Godots that have been made fools of, they see their happy "rival" off.

"What now?" the crestfallen Falardeau asks Godbout, after saying goodbye to Dubois, who is bound for glory and the sun.

"Wait for the film," answers Godbout, equally at a loss.

Clearly, Falardeau cannot bear to wait and cannot tolerate the lack of results, which to him is an expression of failure and defeat. Nor does he admit that the documentary filmmaker's quest to render the past in the ever-changing multiplicity of its meanings can lead elsewhere than to a unified understanding and interpretation – that it can culminate in a narrative that would be accurate in its form and substance at the risk of being complex and many-voiced. Feeling cheated by absence and "absense," the young cameraman, disillusioned with his occupation, leaves his job and becomes a chauffeur for a rich Montreal anglophone. He is disappointed by Godbout's attitude and considers him the "traitor" in the whole business.

This is intriguing. What is the meaning of this insult? Has Godbout been a bad master to his apprentice? Did he lack the courage to finish the project he had undertaken? Did he, despite his apparent resistance, fall under the spell of the model proposed by Dubois, the man of the theatre and pseudo-historian?

THE SUFFERINGS OF THE NARRATOR

Let us imagine a more complex scenario: Godbout is a "traitor" because, in not producing a coherent history of the past and not giving that past a univocal conclusion, he is casting his people – his audience as well as his cultural community – into a kind of identity void without any possibility of a narrative of itself in time, making them prey to the Langoliers, those devourers of identity and presence that leave only a precipitate of what has been, a vague trace of acoustic senselessness that is truly "absense."[6]

In the perspective of *The Fate of America*, the traitor is not the one who has created a fictional history (Dubois) or a disorienting history (Laurier Lapierre) of the Battle of the Plains of Abraham,[7] since these approaches, in spite of everything, are productive of meaning, the raw material of consciousness. On the contrary, the traitor is the one who has failed to take responsibility as a writer, who has left the community with no mirror for looking at itself and dialoguing with itself. The traitor is the one who has failed to enable the community to form a consistent image of itself over time. The traitor is the one who has failed to redeem the community's past through a history that is oriented toward a future to be built, the community in its becoming. The traitor, in short, is the one who has left the past to the dead rather than revived it for the living and the descendants. Godbout, instead of losing his temper at his (former) assistant's insolence, makes light of Falardeau's insult. How is this disconcerting reaction to be interpreted?

First hypothesis: Perhaps Godbout knew from the start that he would get nowhere with his project of creating a new history of the Battle of the Plains of Abraham and that, sooner or later, it would end up in a narrative and interpretative impasse. He is an experienced man who knows what he's doing. After so many novels and films, he is well aware that the reality of the past is to be found in narrative, just as the real man is revealed only in fiction. Godbout knows – and even says so openly – that one must lie to tell the truth about things.[8] It is useless, then, to compete with magicians of plot such as Dubois. Godbout also knows that complexifying the material of the past alters neither founding beliefs nor "mythistories." Why strive then to provide an objective narrative different from the one we already have of 1759? It is impossible to battle history, especially when it is seen as the narrative of the self.

Second hypothesis: By his laughter, Godbout is perhaps admitting that the relationship between fiction and positive factuality is one of completion rather than opposition. Maybe he subscribes to Paul Ricœur's view that human action, to be intelligible, calls for a narrative that would restore its fundamental connections.[9] According to this reasoning, action in one way or another demands narrative. Narrative is not only a consubstantial element of the factuality of action, but also its effective fulfillment. In this view, 1759 is the inseparable sum of what has been and what has been said of it in the past and present. Dubois is as much an actor in the events as Wolfe, Montcalm, and many others have been or will be. Clearly, just as it has no beginning, the past has no conclusion. So why worry about its meaning?

But it may also be that with his (forced?) laughter – and this is the third hypothesis – Godbout is trying to escape one of his culture's heaviest legacies of memory and history. Perhaps he feels we need to put the past behind us. That would not mean forgetting 1759 and the subsequent events that punctuate the great collective narrative accepted by Quebecers of French-Canadian heritage. It would mean abandoning the grievance built on the never-ending recollection of the past, a grievance that obliterates the future rather than opens it up, that makes the descendants the aggrieved rather than the grieving, that stirs up the sediment of losses rather then explores other, equally important, dimensions of Quebec's historical experience. Perhaps Godbout believes it is time to bind the wounds of the past in order to allow the heirs to free themselves from the unforgettable, to seek their own meaning, and to write a new history. In that case, his project's lack of a conclusion would be the redemption of an inconsolable imaginary. What a (hi)story!

CHAPTER FIVE

Toward a Revolution of Collective Memory: History and Historical Consciousness among Quebecers of French-Canadian Heritage

In a little book[1] that presents the most heart-breaking and hopeless view of the Québécois condition,[2] Serge Cantin, the thinker of the perennial misery of the Québécois,[3] suggests, if I understand his argument correctly, that for the Québécois to love and understand Quebec, they must reconcile themselves to the poverty of their origins. They must also recognize the poverty of Quebec itself: material poverty, of course, as a result of the alienating, usurping, and denigrating actions of others against them, but above all, a poverty of memory, as a result of the heirs having forgotten their ancestors' founding action, which calls for contemporaries to take responsibility for the continuity of the legacy of pain and hope of liberation passed down by the ancestors.

At the end of the book, Cantin writes: "The new Quiet Revolution of Quebec will be a revolution of Memory, or it will not be."[4] The philosopher's statement is correct. But the reasoning it is based on is flawed, and the introspective, if not the prospective, horizon his thesis opens for the community, which is tirelessly repeated in the two hundred pages of the collection, is nothing less than devastating and is impossible to endorse.

MISERY AND MELANCHOLY

Reading Cantin's book is a depressing intellectual experience. Not only are the Québécois described with a repertoire of the most pathetic epithets, but they are also depicted as unconscious of their own alienation. Unconscious, first, because they are forgetful of their secular torment and are therefore lost in the limbo of hesitation and decline, incapable of taking responsibility for their destiny and finally transforming themselves from a "cultural nation" into a "political nation." Unconscious, as well, because they are quick to be intoxicated by the demeaning mirage of that falsely comforting materialism from south of the border or across the Ottawa River, a mirage that lulls them with illusions, dopes them with artificial paradises, and diverts them from their historical destiny. Unconscious, finally, but this time in spite of themselves, because they have internalized in their identity the belittling, traumatizing, even insulting gaze of the other, a gaze that still haunts their imaginary and their consciousness of being.

Cantin is, of course, not the only one to express the Québécois condition in terms of tragedy, hibernation, a diverted path, survival in withdrawal, and so forth. This sad view of the past was created by the great French-Canadian and Québécois intellectuals, from Garneau to Dumont, loyally and in good faith – albeit with varying degrees of modulation, subtlety, and complexity.[5] This view of history has prevailed among these monuments of the collective voice less because of the objective demands of the past itself – as if the past could fully determine its narrative configuration – than out of their concern, given the community's acknowledged precarious state, even the potential death of the nation, to establish a moral solidarity with their people.

For these pioneers of historical consciousness, the inherent fragility of the community required that they carry the country as one holds a child. Thus, for them memory had to be at the beginning of method, misery had to structure the purpose, melancholy had to set the tone, and the text had to nurture memory. Unless this circle of identity based on an unforgettable collective poverty – a poverty caused by the other, of course – was closed, the future of the community would be threatened. To forget one's historical condition as a victim would be to have a false self-consciousness. It would also mean risking no longer seeing oneself as a loser. Above all, it would mean, alas!, recognizing that the watchful, accommodating, pragmatic attitude of the collectivity, with its political postulates and consequences that were not very glorious but were very effective, was indeed the cardinal principle of the community's past experience and its envisionable horizon. As if, without suffering, the Québécois would cease to exist, would break faith with what they are and repudiate the original founding place of their supposed identity: "Saint-Sauveur Viarge."[6]

It must be acknowledged that the Québécois have never satisfied those who set themselves the task of conceptualizing them as a community. That is why many thinkers have sunk into a never-ending melancholy, some of them indignant that the Québécois are continually unfaithful to the identity bestowed upon them, others distressed that they do not free themselves from their presumed domination, still others clinging to pleasant daydreams and hoping that they will eventually understand. Although scholarly works that describe the historical experience of the Québécois in a positive light are so numerous they can no longer be counted,[7] there is a reflex that persists among minor and major writers – that of bemoaning the failed or unfulfilled destiny of the community.

In an article presented as an overview of the present and future state of nationalism in Quebec society, Gérard Bouchard, whose importance in the Quebec intellectual landscape cannot be overemphasized, took up in his turn the eternal lament of the unfulfilled destiny and the culture never fully expressed – a lament that seems to both complement and contradict his critical views of the traditional representations of Quebec – as follows: "Some of the most legitimate and fundamental tendencies and collective aspirations are still waiting to be expressed [in Quebec] ... there is a continental dream, an American dream, here that lies dormant, prisoner of our ambiguities and hesitations."[8] This sentence – which is characteristic of a discourse that is widespread if not dominant, and is even considered axiomatic, in the Québécois space of history and memory – remains trapped in the melancholy that overdetermines or inspires the history through which the past is given meaning, coherence, and density. Every word is permeated with disappointment, perplexity, and annoyance at what is observed and diagnosed, that is, the apparently uncompleted re-founding of the Québécois and the ambiguity of their action, or their failure to act – which is nonetheless modifiable provided that certain obstacles are removed. As if the Québécois were desperately angry with themselves for never being or doing as they should and had resigned themselves instead to existing in a perpetual state of collective non-fulfillment. As if their hesitation and their ambiguity, which are obviously disappointing, were not matters to be conceptualized and perhaps accepted, but problems to be solved or evils to be eliminated.

"The tragedy of the colonized," wrote Louis Cornellier in an article in which he in his turn criticized the Québécois' easygoing attitude toward their fate, their memory, and their future, "is that the worse their condition gets, the more lacking is their consciousness."[9] One senses in these complaints the spirit of an eternal observation, one made, for example, by Fernand Dumont about his people almost thirty years ago, when in his book *La Vigile du Québec* he used the following quotation from Ernest Renan as an epigraph: "Let us remember that sadness alone is productive of great things, and that the true way to lift our country up is to show it the abyss it is in. Let us above all remember that the rights of the fatherland are everlasting, and that the little importance it places on our advice does not dispense us from giving it."[10]

Can one, should one continue to conceptualize the historical experience of the Québécois in such a despairing and wounded way, maintaining an underlying hope of magical positive change? When will there be an end to this weeping over the "sleepiness of the giant," to use the words of Félix Leclerc?[11] When will we stop talking about the situation of the community in terms of a failed destiny, an interrupted or diverted path, a confused disconnection, an itinerary blocked by others and by itself, and instead endorse the choices this community has always made and thus help it to recognize itself as it is – that is, as ambivalent in its being(s) – in a process of recognition that could be the means of its true liberation?

It is possible that French Quebec's political or cultural fatigue with struggling and defending itself, if such a mood were to be confirmed, is first of all the expression of an intellectual fatigue on the part of its major and minor thinkers, at least of those who teach, model, and slog away at the historical consciousness of the collectivity, rather that an expression of the community's state of being. To think about the Québécois experience in terms other than those of the trio of misery, melancholy, and re-foundation, which is only the local reiteration of a more general theme, the main terms of which are suffering, lamentations, and deliverance,[12] demands an epistemic rupture that is apparently difficult for those who have the ability, the duty, and the responsibility to speak. That, however, is the challenge on the agenda, because, obviously, the pathetic narrative of the Québécois has exhausted the imagination of those it has always been addressed to.

A REVOLUTION OF HISTORY

There is no doubt in my mind that the future of the Québécois, in or out of Canada, also requires them to form a new relationship with their past and reshape the parameters of their collective history and memory. This task of reshaping the collective path in history and memory – an undertaking that is related less to the production of new knowledge than to the abandonment of a particular perspective on the past and a particular kind of narrative of that past – is, of course, not a simple task, nor one that is easy to carry out morally. And for good reason: it obliges those who take it on to do nothing less than "unthink" their country, that is, to place themselves on the margins of the history of that country as it is generally thought, that country they appreciate and belong to.[13] It also demands that those who undertake it break with an intellectual tradition established by some great writers, the most recent being Fernand Dumont, a powerful thinker whose work has had a decisive impact on the historical consciousness of contemporary Québécois.[14]

To "unthink" the Québécois historical experience in the sense that I mean is to deconstruct and to distance oneself from the themes and tropes by which the past and present situation of this community have been revealed to its collective understanding, the themes and tropes on which the historical consciousness of the community was and still is based. In practice, what does this mean? To penetrate the unthinkable tropes of the Québécois condition is first of all to resolutely tear oneself away from the kind of episteme, filled with depression and longing, misery and poverty, that fuels the reflection of the major intellectuals here, poets as well as academics.[15] It seems imperative that we stop supporting the idea that the Québécois belong to the "proletariat" of history and therefore have a "hesitant mentality," a "defensive reflex," a "fear complex," or a "negative consciousness of being." Not only is this pessimistic view of the community challenged by some historians' recent work;[16] it also poisons any possibility of seeing the Québécois reality in its diversity and its nuances, that is, in its constitutive ambivalence. Furthermore, it makes it impossible to adequately conceptualize the tensions and complementarities – the dynamics of which are often unpredictable – among primary social relationships, the community of belonging, and instituted society, and also among levels and spheres of experience, perception, and interpretation in which actors move, carried along by their good sense as much as, if not more than, by some cultural conditioning. In fact, this pessimistic view precludes taking full advantage of the fertile concept of the community.

Penetrating the unthinkable tropes of the Québécois condition also means acquiring a repertoire of empirical rather than teleological intermediate concepts that make it possible to reveal historical reality in its confusions and ambiguities, its contradictions and torments, its conflicts and hesitations, its adventures and tensions – in its constitutive and cumulative process, rather than in a single-voiced mantra. In this regard, it must be admitted that the concepts of the Québécois "nation" and "people" as they are commonly used, that is, referring to a determining and totalizing reality, are from an analytical point of view constraining rather than productive for understanding the complex reality of contradictory and complementary relationships that exist among the three levels – social relationships, the community of cultural belonging, and instituted civil society – that make up an entity, and largely, but not completely, define what I call the Québécois collectivity.[17]

With respect to the community of belonging, whose existence cannot be denied, it would be in keeping with my views to envisage it as a community of communication and history, that is, a community in constant evolution and in permanent tension with the society it sustains and the social relationships on which it is based; as a community that is neither completed nor uncompleted; as a community whose trajectory is not programmed, theorizable, or predictable; as a community whose boundaries are continually being crossed by its members; as a community that is largely determined by the accidents of history rather than itself imposing its national fate on that history; as a community that exists in an open process rather than in reference to an original seed planted by the ancestors and demanding continuity.

There are many other concepts, metaphors, and images that must be reviewed in order to gain access to the unthinkable tropes of the Québécois past. First and foremost is that of the full-fledged society. This concept, which is closely related to the remodelling of the Québécois imaginary in the 1960s, has, through successive shifts, contributed to a representation – or rather a consciousness – of the Québécois collectivity as an entity that is thought and thinkable in itself, a kind of totality involving practices of convergence, a totality whose past could be traced and that could for this reason be described as uncompleted, truncated, broken, alienated, oppressed, in short, as a culture whose project has constantly been compromised insofar, precisely, as the Québécois society failed to complete itself and remained in a situation of non-fulfillment as a result of the trusteeship imposed by the other.[18]

Envisaging the Québécois historical reality from the perspective of a full-fledged society is a position that is as ideological as empirical – let there be no mistake about it – and it is important to realize what its limitations are. This concept, quite simply, does not provide access to what it aims to represent – the Québécois collectivity – in all its ephemerality and volatility, its twists and turns, its diversity and vitality that have never been fully taken into account, in its relationship *with and against* the Canadian experience, that is, at the heart of Canadianness.[19] This concept also prevents us from seeing the Québécois experience as ambivalent and mobile or, in other words, from seeing ambivalence and movement not as unfortunate digressions but as part of the Québécois experience. In practice, all the concept of a full-fledged society lets us do is document the "misery of being" of the culture, of the Québécois nation, and hence fuel the melancholy of the observer who despairs of seeing this culture, or this nation, take so long in coming into being.

To gain access to the unthinkable tropes of the Québécois past, we could also decisively challenge the idea that this past has always been nothing but a struggle for survival. We know that survival is usually described as a withdrawal strategy of a community that is under siege from outside or undermined from within. Clearly, in this case, *la survivance* is a "hibernation" that coincides with the community's marginalization and results from complementary if not concerted action by the Conqueror's heirs and local lieutenants, the pariah-custodians of indirect rule imposed by the dominating power. But this interpretation seems rather limited. In my opinion, *la survivance* – and I am using the term guardedly – should be seen as an enterprise of community consolidation in the context of the cultural interaction and large-scale migration that marked North America throughout the nineteenth century. *La survivance* was always only one aspect of the community's striving to position itself in the much larger space of Canada and North America, and joining Confederation and subscribing to the Canadian project were equally important aspects. Reducing the Québécois past to a struggle for survival is, once again, only a way of recounting and recentring (or decentring) that past in terms of the metaphor of perpetual crucifixion.

My view of things is different: the Québécois past, if we confine ourselves to one of its key dimensions, that of the quest for affirmation by Quebecers of French-Canadian heritage, has involved a search for an optimal, satisfied, peaceful intermediate position between the spectre of assimilation and that of marginalization much more than a desire to become completely independent or to withdraw into self-effacement. While this search has been marked by what some people persist in seeing as withdrawals, it has been equally marked by victories and extraordinary advances. It should not be perceived as a negative construction of *We Québécois* in terms of misfortune. It has, rather, been a manifestation of the majority's desire to take responsibility for constructing itself as a community in ambivalence by maintaining the trajectory of the collective in the advantageous space carved out by two lines of calculated risk, that of Quebec and that of the Empire, the Dominion, and Canada successively.

I do not intend to expand here on the perspective opened up by this thesis, since it would take many pages. I will say that this view of things forces us to reconsider the conventional interpretation of the community's past from the period of New France to the present, through the rebellions of 1837–38, which never had the decisive effect on the collective destiny that has been ascribed to them, although certain horizons of expectation were indeed suspended or reformulated in the wake of the failure of the rebellions; through the century of the so-called hibernation of the Québécois, which did not coincide with a withdrawal or collective degeneration, on the contrary; through the Duplessis period, which can no longer be seen as the last gasp of the community's backwardness; through the Quiet Revolution, which did not constitute a decisive break by the community with its previous ambivalence; and also through the current project of sovereignty-partnership, which marks the adaptation of the Québécois desire for affirmation to the conditions created by economic globalization, within the framework of a strategic partnership with the other Canadian provinces and the federal government.

Let me make myself clearly understood here: in stressing the ambivalence of being as the central characteristic of the Québécois historical experience, I am not trying to deny that the French-Canadian community experienced domination by the other, that it faced adversity, that it confronted all sorts of irritants, that it knew misfortune, or that it was subjected to more or less pronounced forms of minoritization, negation, inferiorization, and even exclusion. Quite the opposite: the building of the Canadian state and the Canadianization of the country were accompanied by the marginalization, sometimes deliberate and sometimes unintentional, partly successful and partly unsuccessful, of the French fact (as well as the Native fact and the Métis fact).

This being said, the French Canadians' despondency was always only one facet of their overall condition. The French-Canadian community never made the cemetery, or, for that matter, the presbytery, the place of its elevation. Instead it resisted, making use of certain political spaces created by the very ambiguities of the Canadian historical experience. As for the Québécois collectivity, it has always existed by exploiting to its advantage the specific opportunities of its immediate and distant surroundings. Constructing its identity in a complex and changing environment, orienting its development on the basis of the complementary poles of North (the utopia of re-foundation), South (the United States), East (Europe), and West (Canada), it built itself up and advanced overall within a framework of multiple dynamics – polygamy would be a crude but perhaps acceptable term for it – that was often taken for hesitation, confusion, or disorientation, but was always simply the expression of the prudent wisdom characteristic of small collectivities, an unalterable fact for French Quebec in the Atlantic and North American context.

To think the Québécois historical experience in its unthinkable, or at least unthought, tropes, we have access to a great deal of empirical data. What is lacking is the theoretical framework, the conceptual system, the episteme that would make it possible to carry out this enterprise of "re-narration" of the great collective narrative and, therefore, the re-foundation of the historical consciousness of the community, in such a way that the past is past and the future actually belongs to the descendants in a position of recognition *and* distance in relation to their predecessors.

Clearly, the legions of researchers – historians, sociologists, political scientists, and others – who for a long time have been updating the facts of the Québécois past have done an enormous job collecting data and artifacts. In many cases, this has led to micro-interpretations that are not in line with the accepted great narrative of the collective experience of the Québécois. But the authors who have condensed this material and given the great narrative its successive synthetic forms in canonical texts have always repeated, even reinforced, the main framework of the narrative rather than decisively modified it. The narrative is still structured as that of the broken project of French Canada and Quebec.

The fact that Quebec is now presented as a "new collectivity" that has historically built its Americanness in a general movement in four stages – rupture with the old world, new beginning, appropriation, and emancipation (unfortunately partial) – changes nothing. This model remains basically a thesis of collective re-foundation tied to the episteme of lack, a thesis that, of course, is in keeping with the new "paradigm" of the "Québécois nation" – a nation of emergence, not *survivance*, a nation supported by a social project freed of ethnicity, a nation that accepts its constitutive heterogeneity and advocates a civic ideal without at the same time denying its past – but a thesis that does not break with the insidious melancholy of the Québécois intellectual tradition and does not, in my opinion, resolve the complex issue of connecting memory and becoming, past and future.

According to the partisans of this thesis, the salutary emancipation of the community, which they never doubt will come, sooner or later, is hampered – we come back to the vicious circle of Québécois identity – by the uncompleted re-founding of the collective, a re-founding undermined by the Québécois' unfailing self-destructive ambivalence of being, on the one hand, and the incomprehension or bad faith of certain actors, most of them non-francophones, who tirelessly challenge the legitimacy of Quebec's project, on the other hand. Regardless of the individual and collective achievements of Québécois past and present, this culture, this nation, is seen as being prevented from coming into being and realizing its potential, from transcending itself in a kind of deliverance that would finally be its fulfillment. Struggling for sovereignty, the Québécois nation is still on a quest for its founding act. Rarely is the Québécois' ambivalence of being seen as a positive aspect of the culture, as a sign, a signature, even a place of being unique to this culture amid the universality of cultures. Never is it seen as the manifestation of a full, emancipated identity. On the contrary, for most authors, this state of ambivalence is a cultural off-place, even a non-place, an expression of alienation and bankruptcy rather than a mark of lucidity and freedom.

There is in many Québécois thinkers, whose Hegelian inspiration is obvious, an underlying millenarianism that confuses collective reflection on the future much more than it enlightens it. As if the community had taken on a historical mission to move toward a state of fulfillment in keeping with some doctrine on the emancipation of peoples. As if the fundamental, unavoidable, insoluble dilemma dominating the collectivity's horizon were whether to be or not to be Québécois. This millenarianism, which is based on belief and not evidence, results from a very narrow understanding of the Québécois historical experience – a path strewn with obstacles, they say – and a poor assessment of the legacy passed down by the ancestors – one of pain, with a debt of meaning that apparently offers no possibility for the heirs to form a representation of their condition. It also results from the difficulty of facing the supposedly paradoxical option that takes the place of a horizon of expectation for the majority of the community's members, that of simultaneously being and not being Québécois, a condition expressed in the wait-and-see attitude and pragmatic opportunism of the community since the beginning of its history.

If the challenge for major Québécois intellectuals was once to lead the community as far as possible toward a mythic origin, the one that now seems to drive the most influential thinkers is to lead the collectivity as far as possible toward a utopian future – while reminding the descendants of the obligation involved in their heritage from the ancestors, which also, apparently, includes a duty of memory. It was this dialectic between remembering the past and building the future that Fernand Dumont (among others) called for when, in the conclusion of his landmark book,[20] he urged his compatriots to connect what *la survivance* had dissociated, to reconcile the national community with a great political project, and to combine the courage of freedom with their stubborn patience of old.

ON THE DIFFICULTY OF "UNTHINKING" ONE'S (LITTLE) COUNTRY

The difficulty of thinking the Québécois itinerary otherwise than in terms of impediments does not arise out of objective constraints such as the need to respect the integrity of the past, but is primarily a matter of political stakes. Since Québécois pride consists in large part of alienation, and since the narrative of the community's vicissitudes is defined first and foremost as one of resistance, ceasing to suffer and rebel necessarily means ceasing to exist – as if breaking out of this tragic consciousness meant liquidating the past and mortgaging the future. This founding equation of identity has, directly or more subtly, influenced the way many intellectuals frame their thoughts and construct (their) knowledge. In saying this, I do not mean to claim that the Québécois intelligentsia have sold their souls to the powers that be, or to *québécitude*. I reject anys such explanatory platitude. The relationship between the scholar and the political community is far more complex and subtle. It merits being dealt with seriously and dispassionately.

Let me state clearly, in order that there be no misunderstanding, that Québécois intellectuals have in no way abandoned their critical vocation or retreated into ethnic thinking. This being said, it seems that as members of a threatened community, a "small nation" as it is commonly described, many feel bound by a moral obligation to their people to keep their reflection within a space of the thinkable and the "narratable," because going outside it would imperil their community of belonging, a community they are rooted in and have a responsibility to support. This argument is perfectly admissible, and I am particularly sensitive to it.

Fernand Dumont, for one, invoked the inescapable moral authority of memory and belonging over method, and the priority of the ethical building of the political community over the dilettante's knowledge, and suggested that as an intellectual in Quebec he had no other choice than to be a nationalist,[21] that is, that he had a pressing duty to think the (Québécois and French-Canadian) nation while espousing its stakes or, in other words, that he had to express in his analytical and interpretative categories the very conditions of existence and hope of that nation (or that culture).[22] To Dumont, his own critical distance as a modern intellectual was in a sense challenged by the moral solidarity he had to establish with his people, a relationship necessary for the emergence of a historical consciousness that was indispensable to the re-creation of the culture, the place of being and belonging of real people who aspire to achieve universal transcendence against the instrumental rationality of powers, the abstraction of history, and the ideologies of banality.[23] Dumont felt that as a Québécois intellectual he had no choice, in conceptualizing his subject matter and building his arguments, but to reflect *from* Quebec and not just *on* that culture or that place.[24] Thought in exile was to him the expression of a deplorable disconnection between truth and pertinence, a regrettable loss of the memory of origins.

Despite the fact that this position is quite understandable, and despite my recognition of Dumont's genuine humanistic intentions, I find it difficult to subscribe to this view, which assumes a certain intellectual abdication in the name of the urgent need for a culture to survive with a self-consciousness that will enable it to transcend its condition. I persist in believing, perhaps naively, that the role of intellectuals in relation to those to whom it is their moral duty to provide illumination and open up the future – in the sense of clearing the horizons – is to place themselves in a relationship of recognition *and* distance, constantly reinjecting complexity and nuance, and therefore doubt and questioning, those seeds of error, where common sense, fuelled by partisan discourse at times confused with objective reality, spreads only a lot of preconceived opinions disguised as certainties.

Obviously, this position is not without its own moral problems, particularly as regards the conditions of transcendence for (small) cultures.[25] How can one resist the siren songs of belonging and, where appropriate, "dethematize" the representations of a community without denying one's responsibility as an intellectual to contribute to the edification of a collective consciousness that is comforting and liberating for one's people? It is certainly no easy matter to define how the intellectual's practice of reflection and narration can (or should) involve both recognition *and* distance in relation to a community. This is a serious, complex task requiring a great deal of circumspection, good faith, and willingness to dialogue. It cannot be carried out in a detached way in relation to a question emptied of its ethical implications.

A REAL POLITICAL PROBLEM

Why, in general, are the major Québécois intellectuals and their flocks of followers unable to go beyond the horizon of a certain way of envisaging and restoring the history of the community? It would be small-minded and mean-spirited to associate this inability with some base political bias on the part of the learned. The question of the intellectual's relationship to the political community, or the process of reflection and narration that is implied by the interpreter's belonging to a culture, is much more complex and serious. I would like to look at it on the basis of a passage from the collection of essays by Serge Cantin cited above. In one of the pieces in the book, the author writes: "In September 1983, I left Quebec for France. Unlike previous times, not to wander around some area of the country, but to pursue my studies in philosophy at Montpellier. A few days before I left, I had the pleasure of receiving a letter from Fernand Dumont in which, in answer to a rather disillusioned comment I had made to him a little while earlier about 'our senseless country,' I was very politely corrected and reminded of my responsibility."[26] And Cantin goes on to quote a passage from Dumont's letter: "This is not a 'senseless country'; you will have to carry it as one carries a child in one's arms, holding its head up. You must realize that, in spite of the misery around us, you're not alone ... What you lack, perhaps, all of you, is a certain feeling of involvement. Creating that involvement, that solidarity, will be one of your tasks when you come back."

One has to read and reread these quotations, to immerse oneself in the distress of the "heir" (Cantin) and of the answer by the "father" (Dumont), to grasp the importance of what is at stake, which is first and foremost the responsibility of the intellectual in the specific case of a "small nation" or a culture whose situation is precarious, as is apparently true of Quebec.

To Cantin's implicit question (as reformulated in my own words)[27] – How should I as an intellectual conduct myself with respect to this "senseless country" that is Quebec, a country whose meaning escapes me, that I am unable to grasp, that does not let itself be grasped, or that only lets itself be grasped in the ambivalence of its being(s), a trope that exasperates me and that I don't know how to deal with? – Dumont offers an assured, thoughtful, unequivocal answer. His words, as always, are profound and committed. Above all, they are rich in implications and consequences.

The burden he places on Cantin, who here represents the Québécois intellectual, is enormous. Dumont emphatically reminds Cantin that "this is not a senseless country," that this country has sense, that this country can certainly be thought, that it has a meaning. But this country cannot be thought in just any way because the sense of a country, and of this country in particular, is not inexhaustible, and because the boundary between the thinkable and the unthinkable, and therefore between sensible and senseless, meaningful and meaningless, is tenuous, like the boundary separating life and death. Clearly, unless it is thought as it needs to be, this country runs the risk of being badly thought, even unthought, and thus of becoming unthinkable, or meaningless, and disappearing.

For Dumont, there is in the end no alternative, either for the interpreter or for the interpretation of the country. This country, Quebec, needs to be thought by the Québécois intellectual in terms of the metaphor of a child carried in one's arms: as a being that is fragile and incomplete and needs protection; as a being that, still incapable of expressing itself[28] or finding the way to its transcendence in continuity with what it has been, must be put into narrative, and thus given meaning and placed on the path of respect for heritage, by the person carrying it and supporting it, the intellectual.[29]

In relation to their country that is like a child, intellectuals thus find themselves in a position in which involvement, solidarity, and loyalty are obligations. What is more, according to Dumont, intellectuals must carry their country proudly, as one carries a child, holding its head high. Clearly, intellectuals do not need to look at the "little one" they are carrying. Their role is to love; and in that love for their country that is like a child, all the critical tendencies of the "father" vanish. Or rather, they do not disappear completely. Criticism is possible, but its purpose and its stakes must be the education and growth of the country into an "adult" that is sensitive to the demands of tradition and transmission, that is, to the obligations of heritage and those resulting from the descendants' good fortune.[30] When necessary, the guardian's reprimand, full of compassion but without complacency, firmly grounded in a positive, liberating utopian vision, will remind the country that is like a child that it is going astray in pursuing petty, immediate interests, that it is taking the wrong path or the longer one, or that it is no longer progressing in the expected direction in keeping with its potential for fulfillment and transcendence. At no time will this criticism become self-criticism, that is, a challenge to the country's foundations in memory and utopian vision – for that would be to "unthink" the country. Obviously, there are limits to what can be read in the memory and utopian vision of a country.

In Dumont's view, then, the intellectual's mission, at least in a "small nation," is to reassure, enfold, and protect his country and his people as a father loves his child. He must help them to know themselves and especially to recognize themselves, that is, to be able always to find the tropes they need to think themselves lest they cease to exist. The intellectual's role in relation to his people is to carry and transmit their heritage. He is in the position of the father who holds up a mirror in which the child can discover itself.[31] The intellectual, for Dumont, is not in the unconscious (the off-place), but in consciousness (the place). He is the mainspring of a search for meaning in which man, far from giving in to the dark forces of his being, tries to bring them to consciousness. For Dumont, the intellectual, like a poet and *as* a poet, leads (the) being to its own existence, that is, to its transcendence.[32] His responsibility is infinitely great. He cannot rid himself of that responsibility despite the magnitude of the task and the distress he must suffer. Hear the poet's anguish:

> I who am on the other side of words
> Until I run out of breath I must speak
> The other side of the world
> Speak the pitiless silence
> Of those who with their pallid smiles
> Have cast me to the word.[33]

To speak the country, to speak his people: that is the inescapable mandate of the Québécois intellectual.

Should we conclude that, without a "father," that is, without a group of intellectuals who describe the image of the country by relating it to what they see in the mirror, the country cannot be? Dumont certainly says so, at least for Quebec. For him, the duty of the Québécois intellectual is to embody to the world the presumed image of this country he holds in his arms like a child, and that he has a responsibility to love. I say the "presumed" image because the intellectual, according to Dumont's metaphor, does not look at the child he is carrying – he is supporting it proudly, head held high. I say the "presumed" image because this image perhaps does not coincide with the complex reality of the being(s) of the child.

One might well wonder if the intellectual can even ask himself whether the child resembles its image. Academically, yes, without a doubt. But in practice the exercise may be impossible or unthinkable, because, basically, the intellectual and the country belong to the same place. With the people, they form a collective poetics that is the culture expressing itself. If the country is the child of the intellectual, the intellectual, in turn, is the child of the country. His questioning is rooted in the country – because the intellectual speaks from a place – and he sows his answers there, in such a way as to universalize the place of his roots, that is, to fulfill himself as an intellectual and at the same time to create the conditions for the people's and the culture's transcendence.

Between the intellectual, the people, the place, and the culture, there thus exists a oneness of being, expression, and potential transcendence that either comes to pass or fails. Clearly, if the intellectual refuses to construct the knowledge that would make possible the existence and transcendence of the people, the place, and the culture, of which he is the linguistic interface – because "the words are the flesh of the flesh," as Dumont says – then he disappears into the void that he has unfortunately conceptualized, as though being sucked into a space with no horizon (distance) and no roots (memory) – because knowledge is not an idealistic or abstract enterprise. Knowledge is one of the raw materials for building the place of man as distance (horizon) and memory (roots). To construct knowledge that is "inappropriate" from the point of view of the conditions necessary for the elevation of the place of man (for example, knowledge unconnected to the imperatives of Quebec's transcendence as a culture) is to produce "anti-matter," to open nothingness as a perspective – an end, we must admit, that is hardly acceptable, because it destroys hope, virtually annihilating the place, the tie, and the community.

"The authenticity of the political community is the intellectual's concern," as Dumont liked to say. This means that intellectuals cannot resign themselves to being experts or bureaucrats. They fulfill themselves precisely insofar as they move from the world of knowledge, where they only exploit their technical skills, to a higher place, the community of destiny, where they act as participating members. This transition, according to Dumont, "depends on ethical mediation and a set of convictions: that truth is not reducible to verification, but exists on a horizon of values; that the problems [posed and defined] demand commitment as much as analysis; that it is up to the human community and not only the initiated to judge [those problems and that truth] ... Because the political community is both a reality and an ideal; it is necessarily utopian. It is the constantly compromised establishment of a community of destiny amid the accidents of history and the contradictions of factions."[34] Clearly, the intellectual's mission is the development of concrete ties among all human beings. Scholarship is not a dilettante's diversion; it is a social task whose ultimate goal is to bring about an ethical society, the two main demands of which are citizenship and solidarity.[35] "What would we care about a society without a project that citizens could share?" Dumont asks. "What would a society be without the desire for transcendence?" And, answering his own questions, he writes: "It is thanks to culture that humanity frees itself from the monotonous repetition to which animals are condemned, that it enters into a history in which its actions contribute to an accumulation of achievements and an outlook on the future. Culture is thus a heritage. That is why its fundamental issue is that of memory."[36] For Dumont the intellectual is, or should be, at the very heart of this memory, in the obligatory and responsible position of looking toward the future. "Truth is not judged solely by the method that leads to it, but also by the ties and solidarities of the person pursuing it. Truth is the climb toward the universal of Reason; it is also the expression of the unique situations and roots of those who devote themselves to its pursuit and those for whom it is destined."[37]

To maintain the heritage of memory and nurture the utopia of the culture was for this great sociologist the fundamental role of the intellectual. One easily imagines that thinking the Québécois experience in its unthinkable tropes, for example the ambivalence of being, can be delicate, at least with respect to a certain way of connecting the past and the future in a narrative that would be deemed emancipatory for the community. Establishing a fruitful relationship between remembering and becoming is still one of the greatest challenges we can tackle. How can we ensure that the collectivity advances toward a certain transcendence of destiny, a certain ideal of being, a promised or promising land, if the memory proposed to it and the memory the collectivity itself maintains demand that it find its pragmatic happiness in uncertainty, ambivalence, and ambiguity of being – as expressed in all the marks of alienation bitterly attributed to Québécois culture out of rage at the banality of humankind, misapprehension of what is judged from above, or excessive hope in humanity? Similarly, how is it possible for intellectuals to unthink their country – to perhaps shake the foundations of its identity by criticizing, even demolishing, the "themes" of its history, memory, and references – and at the same time to love it – to give it the means to progress by offering it a full and meaningful representation of itself?

Dumont, Cantin, and so many others have in all sincerity always seen only a single acceptable answer to this question. For them, the most justified position demands that intellectuals create the conditions for identity and the common world in a realistic way and in relation to heritage, that is, on the scale of culture. In the case of Quebec, this can be achieved only in a particular way, by carrying the country as one holds a child in one's arms, head held high, and proud of the possibilities of posterity. Québécois intellectuals thus have a nationalist obligation to reconcile their commitment to the world of learning and their commitment to the political community. Nationalism, in this context, is obviously not seen as partisan complicity, but rather as part of an ethic of collective transcendence. This nationalism is basically an expression of dissidence against the loss of shared aspirations. As such, it is the responsibility of the heirs toward the ancestors and the descendants, the ferment of continuity in the midst of constant amnesiac, alienating change. The following passage from Cantin's book, which I quoted above, is unequivocal about this: "Ultimately, I would say that in Quebec one does not choose to be a nationalist: one is a nationalist by necessity, the necessity dictated by the future of one's self in a nation to which one knows one belongs and to which one acknowledges a debt, a nation one would have to be blind or in bad faith to claim is not threatened. Hence we are nationalists, too, let us not be afraid of the word, out of duty: the duty the dead impose on the living to 'reappropriate something of what they have felt in order to make somewhat intelligible what they have experienced,' in Fernand Dumont's marvellous words."[38]

Is there no other option? Is there not, for intellectuals here, a solution to this dilemma of loving their country and nevertheless pursuing a scholarly quest driven by methodical doubt and critical suspicion of utopian visions, wanting to describe the country as it is in its comfort and indifference without being disillusioned by this calm consent, without the naive hope that this condition will suddenly change for the better, without the idealistic expectation of deliverance? Is such a perspective too pragmatic, too boringly empirical? Is the project lacking in colour or appeal? Does this, in the end, mean the defeat of the culture and the collapse of the political community? Is it the abdication of thought in the face of reality, the victory of structure over the work of art? Is it the delegitimization of meaning and the crushing of possibilities? Is it, to put it bluntly, a suicidal horizon for the community?

Is there no way of conceptualizing the Québécois experience that would not sublimate either the past or the future of the community in a kind of beautiful but abstract collective poetics, and at the same time would not mortgage the possibility of progress for the collectivity? In other words, how can a narrative be "for a community," contributing to the community's elevation, without betraying its own requirements for freedom as narrative?

EXPLORING OTHER PATHS

There are, in my opinion, two options worth exploring for discussing the stance of recognition *and* distance that should characterize the reflective and narrative relationship of intellectuals with their culture. The first option takes for granted that, in the case of Quebec at least, it is particularly difficult for intellectuals not to fulfill some civic duty of memory, and thus of *acceptable* re-narration of the country, while at the same time exercising their reflective role and producing knowledge. I can accept this position on one important condition, that is, that the exercise of memory and reflection give rise to a narrative whose objective is "remembering (from) where we're going." According to this logic, the exercise of memory and reflection is not intended to continually bring the country back to its point of origin, to describe it in terms of invariable traits, to give life to its indispensable tropes, to force it to serve an ancestral heritage, or to breathe into it an important destiny, in short, to saddle it with the eternal challenge of being what it was or what one would like it to be – as if what was and still is the Québécois historical experience consisted only of a long process of denaturing.

To lead the country and one's people to "remember (from) where they are going" is to remind them that they were not formed under the influence of a determining teleology but in the circumstances and contingences of the moment; that their future remains just as open as was their past; that their situation is marked by the complexity and difficulty of being and not by the simplicity and habit of enduring as the ancestors of tomorrow; that their horizon is a matter of choice to be exercised and not of salvation to be earned or of a will and testament to be respected. To "remember (from) where one is going," as a narrative shifter, means to find ways to break with an intellectual heritage that puts memory at the beginning of method, and to make this break without ceasing to see culture as memory, on the premise that descendants must, in order to survive, place themselves in a relationship of recognition and distance, continuity and rupture, respect and criticism, with their predecessors.

There is a second option that allows us to avoid the distortion and sometimes the impasse in which intellectuals may find themselves when they are advised to love their country as one loves a child. That option is to reject this metaphor on the grounds that it is the result of a diagnostic error. Quebec is not incomplete and is not like a child that is slow to grow up and refuses its responsibilities. The Québécois' place of historical being is precisely one of ambivalence; this ambivalence is an original characteristic of their path, and the principal one; and going on with it is not a betrayal of the ancestors or the expression of alienation or a pitiful "false self-consciousness," but the patriation of the reflective wisdom of the ancestors in order to build a present and a future defined according to the line of calculated risk, that is, good sense. Unless I am mistaken, this implies "remembering (from) where one is going."

This is not a coincidence. "Remembering (from) where they are going" is perhaps the only way for individuals and collectivities to acquire an active historical consciousness, that is, to become by being freed of the servitudes of the past while still loving their ancestors. Leading the Québécois to "remember (from) where they are going" is perhaps the only way for our intellectuals to think the tropes of the unthinkable Québécois condition, breaking with the episteme of misery and melancholy without at the same time ceasing to love their country and their people, but decisively articulating their becoming, their historical consciousness, their quest for advancement, the culture and the place, the "nation," in a new way. Because it is in the invention of a new relationship to the culture, as memory and as horizon, that the Québécois identity will eventually be redefined.

CHAPTER SIX

What Should We Pass On? Moving into the Future

As I come to the end of this book, I must tackle head-on the question that has emerged in the preceding chapters, and to which I have only given partial answers: How should we convey Quebec's historical experience; how should we translate it into words? How should the legacy of that experience be transmitted to people today? The difficulty inherent in questions of this kind is immediately obvious. To *translate* and *transmit* historical experience is the challenge of interpretation.

TO TRANSLATE AND TRANSMIT: THE TWO PURPOSES OF INTERPRETATION

The activity of interpreting the past demands more than a purely empirical, methodological, or technical relationship to what has been. It implies that from the outset the interpreter has a moral commitment to the continuation of the world and of humanity, a commitment to ancestors and descendants. I will briefly set out my views on this subject.

By "translate" historical experience, I mean assimilate, appropriate, understand, think, and, at the end of this reflective process, bring into being through the activity of interpretation a complex set of facts that are rich in narrative possibilities, that call for tonalities and modulations, nuances and sonorities, atmospheres and rhythms – in short, the meanings of those facts, the meanings they contain, those that will be restored, and those that can be lent them without betraying their essence.

To translate is not simply to reproduce literally or mechanically what is read or observed. To do so would be an offence to the initial author of a text or to the actors in a historical event. Such conduct would be equally shameful for the translator of the text or the translator of the event. Translators, which is what historians essentially are, must reveal and revive. They cannot be satisfied with the role of mere midwives. Could we imagine an interpreter of Brahms who would be content to play his compositions by rote, without any interpretive medi(t)ation? Not only would this make a mockery of the musicality and aesthetics of the empirical sequence of notes in the piece, but the full potential of the music, which was imagined only in part by its creator, would be unexploited, like talent wasted. The whole challenge of translation, like that of writing history, consists in using the appropriate words to reveal both the movement and the effects contained in the original material, whether textual or factual. As André Breton said, the mission of art is not to imitate nature but to express it. It is precisely this duty to express that is at the heart of the work of historians/translators. They play an active, dynamic role in (re)creating the object of their quest. Their process must be based on an ethic of reparation (which should be distinguished from a mystique of redemption). Exegetes, as we often forget, enrich the texts they study and negotiate with through their knowledge, intuition, and interpretations. They reveal the works to themselves, and thus extend them; their vocation is above all not to immobilize the works. Exegetes cannot abdicate their responsibility to maintain a creative intellectual tension with the works they study. Their skill lies precisely in their capacity to turn away from the source of their attraction and, in the same interpretative movement, to exhaust themselves inexhaustibly in it, without closing off its potential for raising questions and opening up possibilities.

To convey what has been, to translate the vitality of the past into words that are just as vital, is a difficult art. And yet it is only one facet of interpretive activity, and thus of the historian's work. Because this past also must be transmitted in the form of a heritage. Without its transmission, there is a rift between contemporaries and predecessors. There is a loss that is not easily mended with meaning. There is, potentially, minor or major dehumanization. There is a diminution of the critical capacity of man in relation to himself. There is also a dispersion of the "capital" of goodness and wisdom, perhaps of hope, and undoubtedly of beauty, that has been built up over time by people reflecting empathetically and critically on their condition, and which represents the most powerful legacy that can be passed on to descendants so that they in their turn can fulfill some of the hopes we are entitled to place in being.

To transmit is not simply to give. Nor is it to pass on the object of one's generosity with no attention or expectation. To transmit is to present, with all necessary ceremony and propriety, what one considers important, indeed essential, to pass it on like the baton in a relay race, with the expectation that the heirs will appreciate, preserve, and build on that legacy and make it an integral part of their heritage. To transmit is to share one's wealth in the hope that it will open up a fruitful future for those who receive it. It should be understood that in this context it is impossible to transmit something that could mortgage the future. That would be irresponsible, even malicious. With respect to the past, one cannot, for example, transmit a heritage of resentment. The reason is very simple: it would wreck the future rather than build it. What should be transmitted is a capital of memories that includes an openness to regeneration and a potential for mourning and even (re)conciliation.

This obviously does not, as I have pointed out, mean cleaning up or silencing whatever may resist preparation for the future. Giving an image of the past that is too harmonious or self-satisfied, ridding it of its horrors, sweeping under the rug the shameful aspects would only imperil freedom. It is said that without memory anything is possible, including the return of old demons. That is true: failing to mention something is in certain cases a crime of omission. On the other hand, memory should not prevent surprising, unthinkable, or indispensable solutions, introduced out of concern for a happy future for the heirs, from becoming, or again becoming, feasible thanks to the words used. It is not possible to divest the remains of the past of the regrets they evoke or the potential for transcendence they offer through their honourable narrative burial by the descendants. How, then, in the context of what has been and what is now Quebec, can we think the past and move into the future?

PUTTING OUR VIEW OF OURSELVES IN PERSPECTIVE

Quebec's history is commonly conceptualized in terms full of accumulated pain: *la survivance*, misery of being, a broken or diverted path, subjugation by the other, blocked development, defeat, stagnation, and so on. Although this seems to be considered obvious or axiomatic, it still raises problems. One may indeed wonder if a narrative of the self so marked by adversity is the best account of what has occurred historically in the space of interaction and reciprocity now known as the province of Quebec, a space whose destiny cannot be understood unless it is seen in the context of the Atlantic system and North America, on the one hand, and the expansion and contraction of the British Empire and the formation of the modern state of Canada, on the other hand. Unless the narrator's objective is to search the past for clues to the legitimacy of the cherished partisan project of re-founding the country as a "sovereign state freed of alienation and emancipated from trusteeship," then the answer to that question is negative. It is negative for reasons not related to the rejection of the political option of Quebec independence, but rather because concepts such as *la survivance*, alienation, impediment, marginalization, and trusteeship do not express the complexity and subtlety of what empirically was Quebec history.

The inadequacy of this sombre, tragic, painful view of the destiny of Quebec and its inhabitants could not be more obvious in light of current historiography on Quebec's historical evolution.[1] In the past twenty-odd years, a whole repertoire of concepts has been forged, discovered, borrowed, recycled, or redefined to translate the particularities of Quebec's development. Thanks to these concepts, which are the result of both empirical advances in research and challenges to and the recontextualization of the Quebec historical experience, we have been able, generally speaking, to get away from the unfortunate representation of Quebecers' historical situation as sad and painful.[2] In light of this work, it appears that ideas of backwardness, retarded or blocked development, withdrawal and self-absorption, enclavement and stagnation, traditionalism and rurality, homogeneity and uniqueness, clericalism and anti-statism, an ethnic class, and *la grande noirceur* of the Duplessis era are inappropriate for describing the structuring and structural dynamics of the Quebec historical experience as a whole.

In fact, the economic and social evolution of Quebec, taking into account the particularities of its history and geography, followed a path nearly parallel and related in many ways to those of other societies in America. Of course, this does not mean that Quebec society was not marked, until late in the twentieth century, by significant differences in its modes of production and lifeworlds. The development of the South Shore and Lower St Lawrence regions, for example, was not the same as that of the Montreal area.[3] Nor does it mean that there were not powerful ethnic rivalries cutting across Quebec society, fuelled by contempt on one side and resentment on the other. On the contrary, the tumultuous and often difficult relations between francophones and anglophones, in particular, are one of the best-documented aspects of Quebec history. Finally, while there is some research that tends, quite rightly, to challenge the province's image as a priest-ridden society, no one would seriously assert that the Catholic Church did not play a key role in Quebec's past.[4]

This being said, the image that is now emerging of the history of the Quebec collectivity has absolutely nothing to do with the paradigm of backwardness, anachronism, folk society, and lack – especially if the collectivity is considered inclusively, with no cultural or political distinctions among its members. Moreover, while it must be admitted that the majority of francophones of Quebec have always, as Canadiens and then French Canadians, been subject to attempts at assimilation, repression, marginalization, and even inferiorization by the English economic and political powers, the fact remains that, generally speaking, they have also been able to play their cards very skilfully, both politically and, for some forty years now, economically. They have been so successful that at the beginning of the twenty-first century, they appear stronger and more assured than ever before in their capacity to be in the world.[5]

Of course, it is possible to make this optimistic diagnosis after the fact, that is, as an interpreter looking back at the insatiable quest for affirmation over more than three hundred years by a community that has become the heart of an open, attractive, and thriving collectivity – which does not mean to say it is without problems.[6] The Canadiens and French Canadians clearly could not have imagined that their struggles, their resistance, their choices, their schemes, their efforts, their compromises, and their stubbornness would culminate in a situation that overall is favourable for their heirs. It is important in the narrative of Quebec history not to downplay the tensions and confrontations that have always marked relations between the group in a general situation of domination, the anglophones, and the one in a general situation of (in)subordination, the francophones. As has been said time and again, in order to open up the future we must not be afraid to confront the past as it was. At the same time, given the current state of being of Quebecers, including the francophone majority, it is difficult to present Quebec history in terms of a repertoire of concepts that mark out an itinerary and an imaginary of misery, impediment, and failure. The fact is that the Quebec collectivity, and in particular the francophone community – which can be called a "people" or "nation" if one so wishes – developed within and beyond the representations provided of it, and the disenchantment expressed about it, by its major intellectuals. It developed not in the meagre space left it by its masters, but in the force of its desire for being, by taking advantage of opportunities that presented themselves and by creating opportunities through the shrewd use of power relationships with and against the "other."

Clearly – and this appears to be the expression of a certain political wisdom – the Quebec community (of French-Canadian heritage) has always been open to the possibilities history opened for it. Even so, it has never yielded to one absolutely negative possibility of this openness, namely its disappearance through exclusion, marginalization, "peripheralization," "secondarization," reduction, diminution, or relegation, on the one hand, or integration, assimilation, absorption, incorporation, inclusion, merging, or imprinting, on the other. Basically, the place of being of francophone Quebecers has always been the centre, or more precisely, that of ambivalence, that is, the capacity if not the political necessity of a community in a situation of objective minoritization to develop in the space created by the tension among elements with contrary and complementary meanings and scope.[7]

Just as the French Revolution expressed its emancipatory project by shouting "Vive la France!" and the constitution of the United States represented the collective American subject in the trope of "We the People," francophone Quebecers have found or created their place and founded their ethical-political project in a pragmatism whose emblematic words are Quiet Revolution and whose political practice is rebellion. It is important to understand the importance of these two (p)references in francophone Quebecers' imaginary and identity.

Rebellion and quiet revolution do not involve a desire for rupture, disengagement, total rejection, or a new beginning. Instead, they legitimize opposition, reaction, insubordination, and sometimes even insurrection, with the ultimate goal not of overturning things or starting again with a clean slate, but rather of re-establishing an unfavourable, shifting, or blocked power relationship on a new basis. In contrast to the revolutionary, who aims to overthrow, the rebel protests, hits back, rears up.[8] Rebellion is a form of resistance to passivity, loss of control, collapse, suppression, annihilation. Unlike revolution, which involves overthrowing or breaking away, rebellion enables a community to situate itself in an acceptable place of being, between positions that are or are considered extreme: for example, in the case of francophone Quebecers (and before them, Canadiens and French Canadians), a place of being situated between the desire for re-foundation and the status quo, between assimilation and marginalization, between the Quebec homeland and the larger entity of the Empire, the Dominion, or today, Canada. Rebellion is not first and foremost an act of foundation. It is rather the expression of a refusal to decide once and for all among possibilities that are considered neither completely good nor completely bad – which contravenes the principles of logic but is not, it seems, incompatible with political reason.

How do (francophone) Quebecers see things now? It seems that between a heritage that is experienced as burdensome (the duty of tragic memory) and a future whose prospects are disturbing ("disambivalence") they are satisfied with a present that is comfortable and reassuring, peaceful and serene, and that contributes substantially to their consciousness of being in the world. Is this a tragedy, a vestige of *la grande noirceur,* a sign of being bogged down, of political impotence, of a sublime and subliminal alienation, of self-humiliation? Is it the sad testimony of historical insignificance and gilded mediocrity that is the fate of a culture trapped in the disconcerting contradictions of its enjoyment?[9]

The answer is no. There is no insoluble conflict between ambivalence and development, even transcendence. On the contrary, ambivalence is an intersection where important things happen that call for serious thinking rather than denial. But in order to open ourselves up to this work of thinking, we still have to break with the Quebec pathos and acknowledge that major new beginnings are not always necessary to bring about what seems just and advantageous.

(RE)PRESENTING OURSELVES

There is another possible point of view on Quebec history, one that is new in some ways and that is largely freed of the defeatist, melancholy, sometimes even bilious foundations of the identity and project of reconquest of a community in the process of becoming a collectivity that fulfills itself in interdependence. This point of view is based on three central categories that are related to history as much as to identity: that of resistance, even attack, and (re)deployment; that of the "maximum integrative position"; and that of fulfillment through seeking and maintaining intertwined ties.

It seems clear that the possibility of such a reinterpretation of Quebec history exists for the rising generation of intellectuals,[10] a generation that has no or little experience of the cultural alienation and economic inferiority that sometimes marked French Canadians, a generation that has grown up, aspired, and learned to dream with the Quiet Revolution, with a horizon of sensibilities and possibilities very different from that of their predecessors, a generation that is able to capitalize on the heritage of old and especially of the last forty years and on a favourable power relationship with and against the "other," a generation that represents the hope of a new world and can acknowledge that it is possible to turn the page of history without in any way failing to show due respect to the ancestors.

This new interpretation of Quebec history that has clearly become possible in the wake of recent events may be described as post-nationalist, but the term is of secondary importance compared to the idea expressed. It is post-nationalist for three main reasons: first of all because it is not part of the customary narrative framework of francophone Quebec's canons of identity; secondly because it does not spring from and is not limited to the nationalist question – discourse, crusade, utopia, and teleology; finally, and perhaps most importantly, because it is needed as a way to go beyond the legacy of the ancestors without disavowing or rejecting that legacy. This interpretation is based on the obvious but difficult to accept observation that the pace of history is faster than that of the healing of wounds.

According to this interpretation, the historical path finally followed by the Canadiens, French Canadians, and now Quebecers has been neither diverted nor broken.[11] On the contrary, that path shows how a population of French culture and heritage, having experienced a failure rather than a beginning or foundation at the start of its existence on American soil,[12] managed, despite the change in its situation in 1763, to stand firm and skilfully manoeuvre with and against English power to carve out a political space where it could develop within the context of a relationship of co-operation and confrontation with the anglophone majority.

Contrary to the customary view, the main goal of this admittedly ambivalent self-affirmation was not the complete disengagement of the francophone community from the larger political entities with which it was associated, willingly or not. Rather, the objective pursued by most of the community's leaders, with the support of the majority of the population they represented, was much more, even at the time of the rebellions of 1837–38,[13] to find a position of integration and maximum autonomy between the appeal of utopian visions and the pressure of contingencies, that is, to resist both assimilation and isolation of the francophone group by the other, which was seen both as partner and adversary. It is in the political space created by the dynamics of maintaining the community's destiny between two options, both rejected – that of incorporation and that of enclavement – that the francophones of Quebec have historically developed as a political community that can neither be assimilated into nor driven from the Canadian landscape.

I certainly do not mean to suggest that defining, defending, or winning this position of integration and maximum autonomy was easy. On the contrary, maintaining the political and symbolic place of the francophones of Quebec within the Empire, the Dominion of Canada, and the Canadian federation – a place English power ardently wished to be that of a minority – has always been difficult.[14] Moreover, it is a struggle that the francophone community has constantly had to reconfirm. This should not be surprising: it is difficult for minority groups to go beyond the need for constant self-affirmation. In the North American context, where there is no demographic or political balance among groups (as there is in Europe, for example), where the logic of majority domination has often pushed aside or driven out minority presences, it has always been much more difficult for those groups not in a position of dominance to exist and develop.

Historically, the quest for reconquest by the francophone group has taken many forms. Determined resistance to assimilation and minoritization is one of them. The quest for formal recognition as a collective political subject and distinct community is another. The pursuit of the status of a majority within the existing power structures is a third. The quest for increased powers, including that of self-government, is a fourth. And so on, from past to present. *A posteriori*, it is impossible to say those efforts have been in vain. The opposite is true. Without that resistance and struggle, those uprisings and insurrections, that risky co-operation and partnership, one might, without lapsing into counterfactual history, suspect that the French presence in Canada would today be the stuff of nostalgia or at best folklore. From this point of view, it is clear that the Canadiens and French Canadians played their cards intelligently in difficult, sensitive contexts, lucidly assessing the possibilities available to the francophone group, whose elites had an interest in promoting the cause if only to maintain and increase their own power. And it should be emphasized that the heirs have always relied on this legacy.

The situation in the 1950s was a major turning point in Quebec francophones' quest for affirmation and their process of development. It was the beginning of nothing less than a new phase in the struggle against English power concerning the place of Quebec and Quebecers in the Canadian landscape. At a time when the concentration of French Canadians and the marginalization of the province of Quebec in the political economy of Canada revived the spectre of assimilation and enclavement (two possibilities absolutely rejected by francophone Quebecers), there was a significant effort, gently in the 1950s and much more markedly in subsequent decades, to counter the constant minoritization of the group in the functioning of Canada and to organize on a new basis without necessarily breaking with the Canadian horizon.

We know now that the battle for and against Canada was waged on two fronts simultaneously, in a way that was both complementary and contradictory, by groups of actors with various ambitions for the future of their respective communities of belonging. On the Canada front, the actions of Pierre Trudeau gave Canadian francophones in the public arena and in federal institutions a new legitimacy, influence, and strength, when they had been losing ground in the early 1960s. Trudeau opened a space of possibilities for the francophones of Canada, including greater symbolic representation than ever before, but this does not mean that all problems related to their recognition and their development were solved – far from it.[15]

Of course, Trudeau's objective was not to promote the development or reorganization of the French Canadians as a "nation" or "people" within Canada. It was, rather, to enable his people, the francophones of Quebec first and foremost, to move beyond their minority status to the reconquest of their Canadian identity, an identity he wanted to (re)shape in keeping with a set of universal values inscribed in fundamental laws. Trudeau also aspired to put an end once and for all to the situation of parallel development of two large distinct communities, French and English, a situation that to him restricted the horizon for his people and for Canada as a whole. Trudeau was not against Quebecers of French-Canadian heritage – that is an abusive interpretation – but he sought to promote their advancement by urging them to put aside the calm ambivalence that, to him, was only the backward, "loser's" reflex of a "little" people that had been stuck for too long in the horrors and illusions of a reactionary nationalism.[16] Trudeau also aimed to prevent (English) Canadians and (French-speaking) Quebecers from returning eventually, unless there were legislative restrictions, to the earlier situation of "two solitudes" – a horizon he considered an absolute dead end for Canada.

Throughout his political career, the eccentric visionary concentrated on this project of promotion of (French) Canadians, which implied, at the same time, a categorical refusal to accept Quebecers' desire for nationalist affirmation, which he saw as regression to a past of misery or withdrawal into separatism. His first step was the enactment in 1969 of the Official Languages Act. The final phase of his crusade, motivated in part by a desire to force his people to shed their ambivalence at any cost – because they did not accept his type of Canadian nationalism readily or completely – was the passage of the Constitution Act, 1982.[17]

In Quebec itself, René Lévesque's actions were also intended to advance the cause of francophones economically and politically. Unlike his predecessors, who had, with varying degrees of success, played the card of the Empire, the Dominion, and then Canada in order to ensure the province's development, Lévesque – like Duplessis to some extent[18] –

decisively favoured Quebec, which, out of a visionary spirit and not out of resentment and vindictiveness, he considered the principal base on which his people now had to build their future. Like his alter ego, Trudeau, and in opposition to him, Lévesque sought to rid Quebecers of their ambivalence in the hope of seeing them break with a horizon of being he considered restrictive and frustrating. His intention was for his people to again become masters in their own house by fully accepting the means and the consequences of the quest for and reconquest of themselves, namely independence.[19]

In light of the clear refusal by Quebecers to back the "extreme" (but not extremist) option he was proposing, Lévesque very quickly revised his position, introducing an idea that was perfectly compatible with the historical (p)references of Quebecers: sovereignty-association. This ideological reorientation enabled him to take power in 1976. To this quiet revolutionary and his comrades-in-arms, sovereignty would enable Quebecers, in particular francophones, to become full political subjects. At the same time, association implied that they were not abandoning their desire to again become central partners and collective actors in the development of Canada, a space and a state that Quebecers had historically helped build and that was also, in many respects, their home. In any case, the idea of sovereignty-association – which would become that of sovereignty-partnership – was supposed to enable (francophone) Quebecers to make the most of their ambivalence of being. As well, it was supposed to lead Canada once and for all to accept the fundamental ambiguity on which it had been built and the structural duality that had always determined its historical path. It is easy to understand francophone Quebecers' enthusiasm for the concept of sovereignty-partnership, an enthusiasm that has hardly dimmed, even now, in a period when Quebec "nationalism" is said to be in hibernation.

What is the situation now for Quebecers, particularly those of French-Canadian heritage? After forty years of continuous recovery and reorganization marked by uninterrupted political action, it is clear that Quebec francophones have created a new power relationship with (English) Canada that apparently suits them and that is not unfavourable to them. It must be admitted, moreover, that this recovery and reorganization have contributed appreciably to making it impossible to overlook the structural dimension of Canada's history, namely the existence of two distinct collectivities living side by side and maintaining relationships of functional interdependence, mutual tolerance, and generally felicitous tension in a web of often disconcerting dissonances.

At the start of the twenty-first century, Quebec occupies a central and unique place in the Canadian federation. The "isolation" to which the province is often reduced, but which, it must be admitted, its leaders also positively seek, only provides quiet confirmation of the special nature of Quebec within the Canadian federation. Up to a point, federal leaders and those in the other provinces of Canada accept this fact although they do not like it, having been unable, despite many attempts, to "put Quebec back in the Canadian box and keep it there." This dialectic between desires and possibilities in the country means that Canada is one of the most accommodating federations in the world, even though the political and constitutional process of the 1980s and 1990s enabled the central government to consolidate and broaden its regulatory powers from sea to sea.

Similarly, despite their minority status in the Canadian federation, Quebecers empirically possess the power of a majority, which considerably reduces the effects of their trend toward demographic decline within the country. Of course, Quebec's central place and its power as a quasi-majority are constantly contested, often in crude, contemptuous ways – which, while frustrating and unpleasant, is an intrinsic part of the political game, if not of federalism.

However, the sometimes contentious nature of power relations between Quebec and Ottawa, the sustained political action of the Quebec government, certain provisions enshrined in the Constitution Act, 1982 (in particular the "notwithstanding" clauses), and the need to make the country work in spite of everything force those who want to solve the Canadian equation to take into account two joint denominators (Quebec and the other provinces) rather than a single common denominator (the Canadian nation) behind the scenes. In practice, Canada cannot progress or fulfill itself without the acceptance and sometimes the ad hoc recognition of its structural duality.

After forty years of quiet revolution, this duality, which has always been at the heart of Canadian history, is quickly changing from an ethnic to a territorial duality. In many respects, the Quebec collectivity is becoming more and more distinctive within Canada, and this is not based on an ethnic criterion. On the contrary, it is founded on the identification of all Quebecers with a single established space, even if that space is primarily and often only greater Montreal, as is the case for the communities that make up Quebec's non-francophone world.[20] Of course, the identification with Quebec is not the only reference that fuels Quebecers' identity practices and imaginary. Their individual and collective representations include many other references, among them the Canadian reference. But it is clear that the more time passes, the more the process of "Quebecization" of the Quebec collectivity is reinforced – which does not imply their abandoning the Canadian reference or, especially, Canadianness.

The "Quebecization" of the Quebec collectivity is particularly evident in the convergence of all Quebecers in certain common features that define the contours of a shared public culture in the province, a culture for which the French language is both the decisive catalyst and the main vehicle of expression.[21] It is also shown in the emergence of a renewed anglophone Quebec literature that takes full advantage, in original narratives, of the themes of greater Montreal from west to east, which, according to astute analysts, is evidence of anglophone Quebec literary writers' openness to the presence of French in the city and to the dissonances created by the contact of languages.[22] The "Quebecization" of the Quebec collectivity is also expressed in the attraction that the culture of Quebec of French-Canadian heritage exerts on cultural currents from throughout the world that are present in Quebec, and in the renewal of the culture's stock of references through dialogue with those currents.

In addition, there now exists among Quebecers of heritages other than French-Canadian a greater openness, a more favourable disposition, toward Quebec than ever before, which could be better exploited for the future of the Quebec collectivity. In practice, the communities that form the "non-francophone world" of Quebec no longer define their interests in opposition to those of the communities that form the "francophone world," in particular Quebecers of French-Canadian heritage.

Of course, there continue to be tensions between the latter and the other communities in the Quebec collectivity. But those tensions are normal and unavoidable in any society that practises democracy respectfully, and they are perfectly contained and resolved by the established political mechanisms. In fact, if the quest for Quebec affirmation – which will not, and in fact cannot, end – was clearly untied from the independence option, there is no doubt that the coming together of francophones and non-francophones around a shared political platform, even shared aspirations, would happen even more quickly. To a certain extent, the independence option, which is perceived as a threat or an irritant by many Quebecers, constitutes an obstacle to the complete realization of the structural duality of Canada on the basis of its new territorial foundations.

This is an unfortunate situation. But it is important to look for the seeds of possibility contained in the affirmation of this duality. If the duality of Canada were acknowledged and welcomed as it should be by Quebec nationalists on one side and Canadian nationalists on the other, this would eliminate once and for all the peril of the eventual disappearance or minoritization of Quebecers as an essentially francophone collectivity in the country – which appears to be the main concern of francophone Quebecers.[23] This would also confirm the status of Quebec – as province, region, and principal home of one of the two major linguistic-cultural communities in Canada – as an open, heterogeneous, thriving, self-assured society, above all a society emancipated from its tiresome old canons of identity.

Of course, this would not resolve the problem of the collective recognition of Quebecers. It is important, however, to assess the situation thoroughly. In many ways, the Quebec collectivity already receives the approbation of governments and administrations throughout the world, based on the implicit or explicit recognition of its identity or other characteristics. It is often forgotten that, although Quebecers do not have a state that is sovereign in all matters and jurisdictions, they have over the past forty years created powerful, effective public and parapublic institutions, including some in the area of international diplomacy. Along with that of Ottawa, the Quebec public service is among the most competent and best organized in the country. It is also the largest, in terms of the number of employees, of all the provincial public services. There is a connection between the relative strength of a collectivity's institutions and the collectivity's capacity to advance and thrive in relation to "others" and in the world. In these terms, Quebec some time ago passed the point of possible relapse to a situation of "existential anemia."

Moreover, as a result of a reinforced presence of francophones in the federal administration for over thirty years now, there is no fundamental obstacle preventing Quebecers from also making Ottawa a place and a means of their advancement as a collectivity that is both distinct and a participant in Canada. Of course, a distinction has to be made between the empirical possibility of such advancement (which, like it or not, can in fact no longer be prevented by any power), and its constitutional recognition (which sovereignists want at all costs, but English Canada rejects).

The fact that any effort by Quebecers to flood into federal institutions would present certain difficulties and frustrations for Quebecers and provoke cries, lamentations, and resistance from those institutions should surprise no one. It is not easy to budge a dinosaur sitting on an age-old tradition. Nor is it easy to redirect the flow of communications or build new networks of power, co-optation, allegiance, sociolinguistic proximity, bureaucratic identification, and so forth. This being said, the task is not necessarily insurmountable. Faced with these obstacles, one must, as a wise philosopher, adopt the attitude of Pierre Falardeau and remember that while the oxen are slow, the Earth is patient![24] It is also important to understand and accept the fact that Quebec is no longer in a situation like that of the 1950s in relation to itself, the federal government, or (anglophone) Canada. In fact, from all three points of view, its situation has changed considerably. Quebecers have a new trope of identity, embodied in the idea of success and performance.[25] They also possess fifty years of indisputable collective achievement. While this success has not yet revolutionized the collective identity – at least as it is expressed in words by those who talk and write the most – it is nonetheless impossible to not take account of it. That, in fact, is what many actors have started to do. Already, at the beginning of the 1970s, a popular advertising campaign proclaimed Quebec's know-how in the slogan "Québec sait faire." And in 1990, when it became obvious that the Meech Lake Accord would not be ratified by all the provincial legislatures, the Mouvement Desjardins, the emblem of "Québec Inc.," asserted that Quebecers had what it took to succeed and that Desjardins had what it took to make their success last.

It was this new, quiet assurance of Quebecers with respect to themselves and the future that then premier Robert Bourassa solemnly expressed on 22 June 1990, following the failure of the Meech Lake Accord, in the following words, which have often been repeated by his successors: "English Canada must understand very clearly that, whatever is said, whatever is done, Quebec is, today and forever, a distinct, free society capable of taking charge of its destiny and its development." Bourassa was repeating, in a more moderate, but also more powerful and confident, and still more convinced and convincing way, the words spoken by Jean Lesage at the dawn of the Quiet Revolution, which were to profoundly mark the imaginary of Quebecers (of French-Canadian heritage): "Maîtres chez nous!" or "Masters in our own house!"[26]

It is, of course, necessary to grasp all the subtlety of the terms used by Lesage and Bourassa in order to understand the substance of their message. It would be a mistake to see in the words of either of the two former leaders of the Quebec Liberal Party any endorsement of the idea of secession, separation, or independence for Quebec. Lesage's "chez nous," although reduced to its narrowest sense in the 1960s and 1970s by those who used it for their own partisan purposes, did not absolutely exclude Canada. In fact, for Lesage, the challenge for Quebecers was nothing less than to reconquer their place both in Quebec and in Ottawa.[27] We have seen how René Lévesque and Pierre Trudeau, in both complementary and contradictory ways, met that challenge.

As for Bourassa's statement, no one who remembers the man could think that in using this rhetoric he meant anything other than the following principles:

- the Quebec of today is no longer the Quebec of yesterday;
- whatever the response of anglophone Canada to the (re)quest for affirmation of Quebec and Quebecers, now or later, neither the province nor the Quebec collectivity can now be marginalized or ostracized from the Canadian landscape;
- the presence of Quebec and Quebecers within Canada is irremovable and their identity, inalienable;
- it is pointless to force Quebecers to endorse a project or vision of the country they do not want.

So what, to Robert Bourassa's mind, was the project and vision that was deeply valued by Quebecers? As one might suspect after seeing the Liberal leader on the Canada-Quebec political scene over many years, he had clear ideas on this subject: given their dual status as minority and majority in the North American and Canadian contexts, Quebecers were above all seeking an optimal position of integration with and against the other, in the hope of carving out a space in which they could thrive and that would preserve them from both assimilation and withdrawal into their Quebec home. Clearly, what Quebecers least wanted was exile and forced isolation, elsewhere or at home.

One may, for various reasons, feel no political enthusiasm or intellectual excitement at such a matter-of-fact statement of position. Nevertheless, the analytical pertinence of Bourassa's pragmatic rather than transcendent view has not been contradicted by the political attitude of Quebecers (of French-Canadian heritage) in recent years. It would be wrong to think that they have rejected their sensible ambivalence of being, which arises not from conservatism or humiliation, we should remember, but from a historical continuity that has served them well. On the contrary, to maintain their cherished option of intertwined ties in the 1980s and 1990s, that is, after Trudeau forced the patriation of the Constitution in 1982, they supported several expedient undertakings, including the Meech Lake Accord, the Allaire Report recommendations,[28] the formation of the Bloc Québécois, and the sovereignty-partnership project. All this activity, while unsatisfying and frustrating in the eyes of many – Jacques Parizeau, for example[29] – did not prevent the advancement of the Quebec cause.

In fact, it seems that, after forty years of quiet revolution and sustained self-affirmation in Quebec, the power relationship between Quebec and anglophone Canada has reached a certain equilibrium – which is not to say symmetry or harmony. Even though Meech failed, the spirit of the accord has crept into the Canadian political landscape and public administration. In practice, regardless of what is said or done, or wanted, it is impossible to skirt the issue of Quebec, as has been clearly shown in the vacillations around the negotiation of Canada's Social Union and the Quebec government's eventual decision not to endorse the agreement. In that case in particular, the "isolation" of Quebec was, in a way, negative proof of the impossibility of solving the Canadian equation without including Quebec. On other occasions, such as when the Quebec Pension Plan came into effect or when the framework agreements on immigration were signed, the demonstration that the Canadian equation was insoluble without the "double joint denominator" was made through a positive process of reciprocal accommodations.

In the long run, if the territorial dualization of Canada continues, as is likely to be the case, the sociological and political reality of the two "majorities" in the country will become so powerful and unavoidable that it will finally become part of Canada's guiding principles. An integral part of the country, Quebec will also in many respects be, de facto if not de jure, both a distinct society and a participant in Canada – which is exactly what the majority of Quebecers want. However, it seems that this combination of Canadian federalism and Quebec self-affirmation, which historically has never been so close to functioning without being officialized, does not please either Quebec nationalists or Canadian nationalists, the most zealous of whom are also, at the time of this writing, (francophone) Quebecers.

In Quebec, efforts are being made to create the winning conditions to bring about what the sociological reality of the province seems to deny, that is, a "Quebec nation" fuelled by a collective identity that encompasses all others and by an irreversible momentum of national sovereignty.[30] It is hoped that this will accelerate the formation of a distinct Quebec historical consciousness in all Quebecers, one associated, of course, with a horizon of expectation focused on the continued development of Quebec through independence. Fundamentally, the objective here is to counter the ambivalence of Quebecers, primarily those of French-Canadian heritage, who make up the majority of the population, so that they will be receptive to the idea of independence.

On the other side of the Ottawa River, the strategy, in keeping with what Pierre Trudeau began in the late 1960s, is to force Quebecers, francophones in particular, to choose between (an independent) Quebec and Canada at any cost.[31] Here the game is double or nothing, relying on the apparent certainty that the vast majority of Quebecers (will) reject the path of sovereignty without a guarantee of partnership – which is a constant in their political tradition and even their political identity. To win the game, federal leaders are relying on two main strategies: using money and symbols to affirm Canada in Quebec[32] and attempting by any means, including legal action, to block or booby-trap Quebec's quest for affirmation. Again, the objective is to induce Quebecers to give up their detested ambivalence of being and unreservedly open up to the only horizon that supposedly is right for them, that of Canada. The federal logic is implacable and unsparing. It boils down to the following formula: the stronger the pressure on (French-speaking) Quebecers, the fewer the choices available to them and the less possibility they have for the political expression of their ambivalence of being.

How far can Quebecers be pushed, or, to use Jacques Parizeau's lobster metaphor – which earned him considerable ridicule – how long withstand the increasing temperature? No one knows. In any case, in both theory and practice, the federalists' strategy of pressure has become so powerful and so taken for granted that for some, probably the least politically shrewd, there is no longer even a question of renewing Canadian federalism in order to convince "recalcitrant" Quebecers to take advantage of the great happiness that awaits them.[33] Regardless of their enthusiasm or naivety, their total lack of political flair or their notorious failure to understand the Quebec identity, the proponents of pressure in favour of Canada have an enormous task. They have to persuade Quebecers (basically the francophones, and more specifically, those of French-Canadian heritage) to leave the perennial place of being of ambivalence and intertwined ties where they have found refuge throughout their history in order to progress and thrive in a complex, sometimes hostile environment in which, although they have manoeuvred skilfully, they have never, either before or after 1759, held a majority or dominant position. We will see what the future holds for this approach of trying to force Quebecers to shed their ambivalence, an approach that is used just as much by the sovereignists as the federalists, their eternal adversaries, and for both with as little success.

THE PAST OF THE FUTURE, AND THE FUTURE OF THE PAST

At the dawn of the twenty-first century, Quebec's future can no longer be envisaged on the basis of a discourse and an episteme that fail to acknowledge the tremendous changes that have taken place in Quebec in the last forty years, that challenge the potential for fulfillment offered to Quebecers by intertwined ties with both Canada and Quebec, and that present Canada as an obstacle to Quebecers' development rather that an additional springboard to growth.

It is in ambivalence that Canadiens, French Canadians, and Quebecers have advanced historically, between the possibilities offered to them and those they themselves have created through their struggles. This ambivalent itinerary, both imposed and sought, has not led to a collective failure or a deviation of destiny – on the contrary. While the experience of Quebec and Quebecers (of French-Canadian heritage) in the context of Canada has been marked by many frustrations and obstacles, it has also proven to be full of possibilities and advances. The challenge for observers is not to deny or denigrate the structural and structuring presence of ambivalence of being in Quebecers' past. Rather, it is, by acknowledging this reality without endorsing it, to bring out its advantages and limitations, taking into account in the analysis of every situation the possibilities offered to the community by the power relationships in which it has necessarily become involved. The goal of such an analysis, it should be noted, is not to dispute that independence may one day be an option chosen by the Quebec collectivity. It is more a matter of showing that this eventuality is not a logical, necessary, or predestined culmination of Quebecers' past experience.

It may well be that this position is the one to which most Quebecers finally rally. Unlike the proponents of the sovereignist option, the vast majority of Quebecers do not see independence as a historical necessity or a redemptive utopia. Rather, they see the *idea of independence*, which they flirt with but avoid embracing, as a means of maintaining an optimal power relationship with and against anglophone Canada. It is this fact, so obvious to the observer who listens instead of condemning, that the supporters of Quebec independence refuse to accept, that federal leaders, in particular prominent Quebecers in the Liberal Party of Canada, reject out of ideological fixation, and that anglophone Canada, caught in the trap of its own myths and symbols of identity while offering nothing but empty responses to the Quebec vision of Canadian identity, is condemned to neither see nor understand.

It is possible to write a history of Quebec that is lucid and unsparing about what has been but that nevertheless focuses on the achievements of the past, and that does not lead to melancholy, doubt, or worry, nor necessarily to separation. It is equally possible to rethink the country in a way that resolves its current dissonances through a process of reciprocal clarifications by the actors involved. Contrary to what is claimed by the legions of the resigned, whose demoralizing or unrealistic views promote despair,[34] the Canadian "sickness" is not some kind of incurable cancer that objectively marks the condition of the country. It is the result, primarily, of the refusal by decision-makers to commit themselves in good faith to the search for responsible and original accommodations between the federalist project of Canadians, some of whom are also Quebecers, and the quest for affirmation by Quebecers, which is not incompatible with the existence of a reunited Canada. This refusal is symptomatic of something that, beyond their apparent discord, is shared by sovereignists and federalists alike: an inability to accept the healthy complexity and interrelation of empirical situations, an abdication in the face of the key challenge of politics to transform problems into projects.

There remains, as a liberating horizon, the obligation to think the unthinkable and to do the impossible. In keeping with the general philosophy of this book, that is a heritage that can be passed on to the descendants.

Notes

CHAPTER ONE

1 In April 1995, thirty years after the publication of the report of the *Royal Commission of Inquiry on Education in the Province of Quebec* (Parent Report), the government of Quebec established the Estates General on Education to review and update the achievements of that very important commission of inquiry which revolutionized the education system in Quebec in the 1960s. The purpose of the Estates General was to give (back) a voice to groups and individuals and allow them to express their ideas on the problems and possible reforms of the province's education system.

2 Quebec, Ministère de l'Éducation, *Learning from the Past: Report of the Task Force on the Teaching of History* (Quebec City: Ministère de l'Éducation, May 1996).

3 In a little book published in the mid-1980s, French historian Marc Ferro pointed out that this preoccupation with history exists in all societies in the world: *L'histoire sous surveillance. Science et conscience de l'histoire* (Paris: Calmann-Lévy, 1985). See also his *The Use and Abuse of History, or, How the Past is Taught* (London

and Boston: Routledge & Kegan Paul, 1984, c1981), translation of *Comment on raconte l'histoire aux enfants à travers le monde entier* (Paris: Payot, 1981).

4 Josée Legault, "Histoire d'exister," *Le Devoir,* 17 July 1996; Béatrice Richard, "Se souvenir et devenir, ou oublier et disparaître?" *Le Devoir,* 25 August 1996; Louis Cornellier, "Comment peut-on être Québécois pure laine?" *Le Devoir,* 7–8 September 1996; Jean-Marc Léger, "L'histoire nationale révisée à l'aune du multiculturalisme," *Bulletin d'histoire politique* 5, no. 1 (fall 1996): 59–63; Marc-Aimé Guérin, *La faillite de l'enseignement de l'histoire (au Québec)* (Montreal: Guérin, 1996).

5 Jacques Dagneau, "Une vision dépassée de l'histoire. Réponse à Josée Legault," *Le Devoir,* 29 July 1996; Gonzalo Arriaga and Éric Normandeau, "Vous avez dit 'québécitude'? Réponse à Louis Cornellier," *Le Devoir,* 28–29 August 1996.

6 Since the beginning of the 1980s, the teaching of history in Quebec had been almost non-existent in elementary school, and in high school consisted of only two compulsory courses, one in general history (in the second year) and the other in national history (in the fourth year), as well as an elective course on twentieth-century history (in the fifth year). In keeping with the recommendations of the Task Force on the Teaching of History, students in the first two years of elementary school will have at least three hours of compulsory instruction in the social sciences each week; in the second and third years of elementary school, this will increase to five hours of weekly instruction. In high school, one history course will be compulsory each year, making a total of five courses in high school. At the college level, finally, students in pre-university education will be required to take one history course.

7 The use of the word *generally* is deliberate, because this is not always the case. In fact, sometimes, the relationship francophone Quebecers of French-Canadian heritage establish with the world and with themselves as a community draws on a more positive view of their condition and a more glorious memory of their past. This said, francophone Quebecers remain fundamentally stuck in a kind of dialectic of past and present for which they find

no solution in either politics or memory, and which may be expressed in terms of three dilemmas: to open up to the other while avoiding losing themselves; to express their emancipation while remembering their alienation; to redefine the group identity without concealing its historical attributes. On this subject, see J. Létourneau and Jacinthe Ruel, "Nous Autres les Québécois. Topiques du discours franco-québécois sur Soi et sur l'Autre dans les mémoires déposés devant la Commission sur l'avenir politique et constitutionnel du Québec," in *Mots, représentations. Enjeux dans les contacts interethniques et interculturels,* ed. Khadiyatoulah Fall, Daniel Simeoni, and Georges Vignaux (Ottawa: Presses de l'Université d'Ottawa, 1994), 283–307.

8 The collective memory of francophone Quebecers of French-Canadian heritage has been extensively studied and its central themes traced and associated with the formation of the group identity. There has also been increasing interest in the gaps and shadowy zones in that memory, which is making it possible to slowly bring to light the repressed aspects of the identity. But, at least until now, the question of how it is possible to forget while remembering, that is, how to live with the memory of the past without being obliterated by its stamp and its burden, has been practically untouched. One exception to this general silence, which I will comment on later, is Gérard Bouchard, *La Nation québécoise au futur et au passé* (Montreal: VLB, 1999).

9 I would like to remind the reader that Quebec's motto, which has appeared on the licence plates of all vehicles registered in Quebec since 1976, is "Je me souviens" (the title of this article is a play on words on this expression). Although it has been used as a slogan since 1883, it was only in 1939 that it appeared officially under the province's coat of arms. Attributed to Eugène-Étienne Taché, the designer of the legislative building in Quebec City, the phrase "Je me souviens" remains largely enigmatic. It is a quotation from the first line of a poem that, for some people, expresses the ambivalent allegiance of the Canadiens with respect to France and Great Britain, and which reads: "Je me souviens d'être né sous le lis et d'avoir grandi sous la rose" ["I remember having been born under the lily and growing up under the rose"]. For others, who

are perhaps more pragmatic and realistic, this slogan simply expresses Taché's personal views on the history of Quebec as a distinct province in confederation. On the anecdotal history of Quebec's motto, see Gaston Deschênes, *Les symboles d'identité québécoise* (Quebec City: Assemblée nationale, 1990).

10 It is obviously deplorable that history as it is taught in Quebec schools has never broken its ties with the political and national concerns of many people involved in education, but the fact is that this tendency is universal. History, as Marc Ferro points out, is everywhere "under scrutiny."

11 "La fonction sociale de l'histoire," *Histoire sociale*, no. 4 (November 1969): 16 (translators' note: our translation). Since I will be in continual dialogue with Dumont in this book, it is essential that I give some indication of his enduring importance in Quebec's intellectual landscape despite his death in May 1997. A professor of sociology at Université Laval, poet, man of action, and leading intellectual in Quebec for more than thirty years, Fernand Dumont was a major thinker on Quebec identity and one of the important theorists of culture in the international francophone world. Author of an outstanding body of work, he has written some genuine classics, including *Le lieu de l'homme* (1968), *Le sort de la culture* (1987), and *Genèse de la société québécoise* (1993). To get a sense of Dumont's importance, see Jean-François Warren, *Un supplément d'âme. Les intentions primordiales de Fernand Dumont* (Quebec City: Presses de l'Université Laval, 1998); Serge Cantin, ed., *Fernand Dumont, un témoin de l'homme* (Montreal: L'Hexagone, 2000); "Mémoire de Fernand Dumont," ed. Jean-Philippe Warren and Simon Langlois, special issue of *Recherches sociographiques* 42, no. 2 (2001); "Présence et pertinence de Fernand Dumont," ed. Serge Cantin and Stéphane Stapinsky, special issue of the *Bulletin d'histoire politique* 9, no. 1 (fall 2000).

12 In defence of the authors of the report, it should be pointed out that their position with respect to the designation of Quebec as a culturally plural society was amply supported by the briefs submitted to the commission.

13 Josée Legault was an advisor to Premier Bernard Landry. She had previously been a columnist for *Le Devoir* and the *Montreal*

Gazette. Associated with the radical wing of the Parti Québécois, she has often taken strong positions on questions concerning the future of Quebec. She has written several books, including *L'invention d'une minorité: les Anglo-Québécois* (Montreal: Boréal, 1992).

14 André Turmel, "Le devoir de mémoire," *Le Devoir*, 28 June 1996 (translators' note: our translation). Turmel was replying to an article by Marc Angenot ("50% des voix plus une," *Le Devoir*, 13 June 1996), in which the author had harshly criticized what he felt was a deplorable complicity between francophone Quebec intellectuals, including journalists, and the political leadership, particularly sovereignists. (Angenot's counter-thrust to his critics was "La 'démocratie à la québécoise': les intellectuels nationalistes et la pensée unique," *Le Devoir*, 19 July 1996). In his review of the original French version of this book, Angenot again turned to the question of the relationship of the (francophone) Quebec intellectual to the "Quebec nation," but took a less categorical position. The calm debate between him and myself may be read in *Spirale* 180 (September–October 2001): 14–17.

15 This "memoriogram," a veritable memo of predetermined memory, has been used countless times to reply to someone who has "offended" or to bolster a rather uncertain historical consciousness with facts and dates. There is, for example, then minister Bernard Landry's rejoinder to Lise Thibault (who was about to become lieutenant-governor of Quebec) following the honourable lady's declaration concerning the good fortune of Quebecers to have been under the sovereignty of England rather than of France: "To say that is to forget all the attempts at assimilation by the British Crown and its agents. It is to forget the *patriotes* of 1837, the violent confrontations, and the hangings and exiles. It is to forget the Act of Union, which forced Quebec to unite with Ontario when Ontario was in debt, putting us in debt at the same time. The Act of Union by which they made us lose our majority by merging with a larger entity. It is to forget the Durham Report. It is to forget the decision of the Privy Council that amputated Labrador from Quebec." And the minister recommended that Her Excellency "refresh her memory, go back to her history books

and devote her free time to reading Brunet, Séguin, Lacoursière, Vaugeois, Lamarche, and others": reported by Pierre O'Neil, "Le bienfait de la conquête anglaise," *Le Devoir,* 25–26 January 1997 (translators' note: our translation). The chronological reminder by the Regroupement des historiens et historiennes pour le Oui (Historians in favour of a "yes" vote) published in the *Bulletin d'histoire politique* 4, no. 3 (spring 1996): 93–4, should also be mentioned. Finally, more recently, there was the "history lesson" given by Gérard Bouchard to John Ralston Saul, pointing out the latter's historical errors and oversights: "La vision siamoise de John Saul," *Le Devoir,* 15–16 and 17 January 2000. Saul's reply was not long in coming: John R. Saul, "Il n'y a pas de peuple conquis," *Le Devoir,* 22 and 24 January 2000. Others later contributed to the discussion: Jean Larose, "Pas d'histoire," *Le Devoir,* 5 February 2000; Jocelyn Létourneau, "Des histoires du passé," *Le Devoir,* 12 February 2000.

16 This is a reference to the words of René Lévesque the night of the defeat of the first referendum, on sovereignty-association, on 20 May 1980. Speaking to a disheartened crowd gathered in the Paul-Sauvé Arena in Montreal, the leader of the Parti Québécois and premier of Quebec, a moderate man and an irreproachable democrat, said: "If I understand correctly, what you are saying to me is 'until the next time'" (translators' note: our translation).

17 "J'ai tant besoin du 24 juin," *Le Devoir,* 23 June 1997. Author of a substantial body of literary work, Victor-Lévy Beaulieu is one of the most important popular writers of contemporary Quebec.

18 *The Fate of America,* subtitles by Robert Gray (Montreal: National Film Board of Canada, 1997), translation of *Le Sort de l'Amérique* (Montreal: National Film Board of Canada, 1996). Script published in French as *Le Sort de l'Amérique* (Montreal/Paris: Boréal/K-Films, 1997), 26.

19 *L'ingratitude. Conversation sur notre temps,* with Antoine Robitaille (Montreal: Québec-Amérique, 1999), p. 137 (translators' note: our translation).

20 Objectively in the sense that one is always more or less culturally determined by the particularities of one's place and one's origin, socialization, and education.

21 *L'avenir de la mémoire* (Quebec City: Nuit blanche, 1995), 58 (translators' note: our translation).

22 On this subject, see Hans Jonas, *The Imperative of Responsibility: In Search of an Ethics for the Technological Age* (Chicago: University of Chicago Press, 1984), translation of *Le principe responsabilité* (Paris: Cerf, 1990 [1979]), ch. 4, point 5.

23 These great intellectuals who in various periods formed the French-Canadian imaginary and episteme include François-Xavier Garneau, Lionel Groulx, Guy Frégault, Michel Brunet, Maurice Séguin, and Fernand Dumont; they explicitly played the role of thinkers and not only scholars. See the following works in particular: Jean Lamarre, *Le devenir de la nation québécoise selon Maurice Séguin, Guy Frégault et Michel Brunet (1944–1969)* (Sillery: Septentrion, 1993); Ronald Rudin, *Making History in Twentieth Century Quebec* (Toronto: University of Toronto Press, 1997); Serge Gagnon, *Quebec and Its Historians, 1840 to 1920* (Montreal: Harvest House, 1982); Yvan Lamonde, *Histoire sociale des idées au Québec, 1760–1896* (Montreal: Fides, 2000).

24 For an illustration, see J. Létourneau and Sabrina Moisan, "Young People's Assimilation of a Collective Historical Memory: A Case Study of Quebecers of French-Canadian Heritage," in *Theorizing Historical Consciousness*, ed. Peter Seixas (Toronto: University of Toronto Press, forthcoming).

25 On this subject, see J. Létourneau, "La production historienne courante portant sur le Québec et ses rapports avec la construction des figures identitaires d'une communauté communicationnelle," *Recherches sociographiques* 36, no. 1 (1995): 9–45.

26 For a recent example of this reflex, see Jean-François Lisée, *Sortir de l'impasse. Comment échapper au déclin du Québec?* (Montreal: Boréal, 2000).

27 Jean-Jacques Simard, "L'identité comme acte manqué," *Recherches sociographiques* 36, no. 1 (winter 1995): 103–11, in which the author uses the expression "rebelles manqués."

28 *L'avenir de la mémoire*, 55 (translators' note: our translation).

29 On this subject, see Emmanuel Kattan, *Penser le devoir de mémoire* (Paris: Presses universitaires de France, 2002).

30 Disenchanted with the political situation in Quebec, which according to her was marked by apathy and indifference, stagnation, and the eternal return of the same problems and the same solutions, Hélène Jutras, then a law student at McGill University, published a resounding article in *Le Devoir* on 30 August 1994 ("Le Quebec me tue" [Quebec is killing me]), which generated the largest volume of mail ever received by the paper. Following the publication of several letters against her position, Jutras came back with another letter with an equally provocative title, "Oui, le Québec me tue" (Yes, Quebec is killing me), (*Le Devoir,* 27 September 1994). Jutras's texts were collected and published in English under the title *Quebec Is Killing Me* (Kemptville, Ont.: Golden Dog Press, 1995). It seems that, since her public departure in the mid-1990s, Ms Jutras has gone through a major "(r)evolution" in her personal life and ideas (see "Le Québec ne l'a pas fait mourir" [Quebec didn't kill her], *Le Devoir,* 10 August 1999).

31 Serge Cantin, *Ce pays comme un enfant* (Montreal: L'Hexagone, 1997), 189 (translators' note: our translation).

32 Formulation borrowed from Serge Cantin, "Fernand Dumont: la mort d'un homme de parole et d'action," *Le Devoir,* 10–11 May 1997.

33 The reader should bear in mind that in this book I am using the term *historian* to mean a member of the community of men and women who do scholarly work – that is, systematic and rigorous work – in the study of the past, whatever their specific disciplines.

34 We know that the history we compose of the past is always the product of a complex dialectic made up of factual recollections and forgettings that share a common boundary within a single semio-narrative structure that refers somewhere to competing powers. From this point of view, forgetting is not necessarily conscious concealment of the past, but the automatic result of the fact that recollection simultaneously creates both the thinkable (remembering) and unthinkable (forgetting). This is why remembering necessarily implies that one forgets as well. In this context, what is forgotten may be defined as a memory that is not activated and that may resurface if the memory covering it

disappears or the boundary between recollection and forgetting is broken down as a result of critical reflection leading to the deconstruction of a particular cultural modelling of memory.

35 Several gems are cited in *Trou de mémoire*, the transcription of a series of broadcasts on Radio-Canada from 9 July to 27 August 1995 (Montreal: SRC-Radio, 1995).

36 I am not claiming, because I am unable at this time to demonstrate it rigorously on the basis of a broad corpus, that these essays, which were collected as an informal classroom exercise, are representative of the historical memory of francophone Quebecers. My intuition, however, is that they are, for two reasons: first of all, because they repeat essentially what is said in the public arena about francophone Quebecers' past; and secondly, because year after year I find essentially this view of Quebec history among students interviewed. Two recent studies confirm my impression: Sabrina Moisan, "La mémoire historique de l'aventure québécoise chez les jeunes Franco-Québécois d'héritage canadien-français. Coups de sonde et analyse des résultats" (master's thesis, Université Laval, 2002); Jacques Caouette, "Les représentations des élèves de quatrième secondaire de la Polyvalente Le Carrefour de Val-d'Or concernant l'histoire" (master's thesis, Université du Québec en Abitibi-Témiscamingue, 2000). (Translators' note: our translation of student essays.)

37 *Act respecting the future of Québec (Bill 1)* (Quebec City: Éditeur officiel du Québec, 1995), preamble. The bill includes a declaration of sovereignty.

38 These dates correspond to the following events: 1759 (conquest of New France by the British); 1763 (formal cession of New France to Great Britain by France); 1774 (Quebec Act); 1837–38 (*patriote* rebellions crushed by British forces); 1840 (Act of Union of the two Canadas); 1867 (British North America Act); 1917 (conscription); 1942 (conscription); 1982 (patriation of the Canadian Constitution without Quebec's agreement); 1990 (failure of the Meech Lake Accord); 2001 (passage of the Clarity Act, federal law on the requirement for clarity in a referendum).

39 Louis Cornellier, "Plaidoyer pour l'idéologie tabarnaco," *Le Devoir*, 4 July 1996. For a discussion of *la survivance* see chapter 5.

40 I would not dare suggest that this narrative also fuels their political imaginary, although this is taken for granted – too readily – by many observers. My feeling is that there is a growing gap between the narrative of identity and memory circulating in the public space – a narrative that people often make their own, almost always uncritically – and the political imaginary to which people aspire. This appears to be particularly true among young people, whose representations – that of the nation, for example – seem to differ substantially from those of their parents. See J. Létourneau, "La nation des jeunes," in *Les jeunes à l'ère de la mondialisation. Quête identitaire et conscience historique*, ed. Bogumil Jewsiewicki and J. Létourneau, with Irène Herrmann (Sillery: Septentrion, 1998), 411–30.

41 Far be it from me to claim that this is not taking place. Historians are undertaking it in part, and so are members of the literary community. But the malaise of Quebec memory is deep, the struggle against demagoguery and bad faith is unequal, and the weight of politics is so crushing in any discourse on Quebec's past that the transmutation of memory is slow and difficult. For a position that has much in common with mine, see Pierre Nepveu, "Notes sur un angélisme au pluriel," and "L'impossible oubli," in *Le Devoir,* 9 and 10 June 1997.

42 Discussed in Gilles Bibeau, "Tropismes québécois. Je me souviens dans l'oubli," *Anthropologie et sociétés* 19, no. 3 (1995): 151–2.

CHAPTER TWO

1 "Revisionism and the Search for a Normal Society: A Critique of Recent Quebec Historical Writing," *Canadian Historical Review* 68, no. 1 (1992): 30–61.

2 It would take too much space to cite all the relevant work. The most spectacular work by members of the CIEQ may be found in the Quebec historical atlas project, which Serge Courville, Jean-Claude Robert, and Normand Séguin are associated with.

3 Louis Rousseau and Frank W. Remiggi, *Atlas historique des pratiques religieuses* (Ottawa: Presses de l'Université d'Ottawa, 1998).

4 See Alain G. Gagnon and Michel Sarra-Bournet, ed., *Duplessis. Entre la grande noirceur et la société libérale* (Montreal: Québec-Amérique, 1997); Jacques Beauchemin, Gilles Bourque, and Jules Duchastel, *La société libérale duplessiste* (Montreal: Presses de l'Université de Montréal, 1995); Gilles Paquet, *Oublier la Révolution tranquille* (Montreal: Liber, 1999); "Le chaînon manquant," special issue of *Société* [Montreal] 20/21 (summer 1999).

5 See, for example, Yvan Lamonde's interviews with Claude Montpetit, "Défaire le nœud des héritages," *Le Devoir*, 22 November 1998, and Gil Courtemanche, "Un peuple entre deux chaises," *L'Actualité*, 1 April 1997, 56–8.

6 "Pour décloisonner notre réflexion collective," *Le Devoir*, 24 November 1997; "Nationalisme ethnique, avez-vous dit?" *Le Devoir*, 1–2 June 1996; "Une francophonie nord-américaine," *La Presse*, 7 May 1998; "Manifeste pour une coalition nationale," *Le Devoir*, 4 September 1999; "Contrer la pensée dichotomique," *Le Devoir*, 5 April 2001; "La co-intégration. Refonder la nation dans le pluralisme," *Le Devoir*, 6 April 2001; "Pourquoi fêter?" *La Presse*, 23 June 2001.

7 "Ouvrir le cercle de la nation. Activer la cohérence sociale," *L'Action nationale*, 87, no. 4 (April 1997): 107–37.

8 *Mitsouk* (Montreal: Boréal, 2002). Reviews of this book include Louis Cornellier, "Le grand roman de l'américanité québécoise," *Le Devoir*, 8 June 2002.

9 On Quebec historiography, see Serge Gagnon, *Quebec and Its Historians: 1840–1920* (Montreal: Harvest House, 1982); ibid., *Quebec and Its Historians: The Twentieth Century* (Montreal: Harvest House, 1985); Ronald Rudin, *Making History in Twentieth-Century Quebec* (Toronto: University of Toronto Press, 1997).

10 G. Bouchard, *La Nation québécoise au futur et au passé* (Montreal: VLB, 1999); ibid., "Le souci de l'actuel: deux clés pour la réécriture de l'histoire nationale," paper presented at the conference "Giving the Past a Future," McGill Institute for the Study of Canada, McGill University, January 1999; Gérard Bouchard and Michel Lacombe, *Dialogue sur les pays neufs* (Montreal: Boréal, 1999), chap. 10 in particular.

11 G. Bouchard, "Conclusion générale: La nation comme imaginaire et comme réalité," in *La nation dans tous ses états. Le Québec en comparaison*, ed. Yvan Lamonde and G. Bouchard (Montreal: L'Harmattan, 1997), 349.

12 G. Bouchard, "La réécriture de l'histoire nationale au Québec. Quelle histoire, quelle nation?" in *À propos de l'histoire nationale*, ed. Robert Comeau and Bernard Dionne (Sillery: Septentrion, 1999), 127.

13 For Bouchard, the nation is as much a cultural as a civic entity – hence the qualifier "sociological." For him, the nation is equivalent to a project of collective development, common values, and collective mobilization, in short, everything that is good, right, and just – and not too ethnic. In a sense, Bouchard's (sociological) Quebec nation is comparable to Trudeau's Canadian nation, which he himself acknowledges. So why recreate a smaller version of what already exists? "Because," says Bouchard, "Canada has never been able to accommodate the two major linguistic communities, francophone and anglophone, in a single ideal and a single entity. Nor has Canada succeeded in providing the conditions that would have enabled Quebec to develop fully as a nation and as a responsible francophone society. To call for sovereignty for Quebec is simply to acknowledge this ongoing inability, which has repeatedly been demonstrated" (*La nation québécoise au futur et au passé*, 76 [translators' note: our translation]).

14 G. Bouchard, "Qu'est-ce qu'une nation?" in *Nationalité, citoyenneté et solidarité*, ed. Michel Seymour (Montreal: Liber, 1999), 465–78.

15 It is difficult to determine from the works discussed here whether Bouchard goes as far as considering the nation as "the principle of totalization of social relationships in a space-time configured in national forms" (Gilles Bourque; translators' note: our translation). I would be tempted to answer in the affirmative. In this case, and despite the caveats with which Bouchard punctuates his work, his interpretative project seems to consist only of giving a historical and prospective dimension to the tautology of the nation in which his scholarly thought and civic action are rooted.

16 The attentive reader will have noticed several shifts, even confusions, between the Quebec collectivity, the Quebec nation, the (francophone) Quebec collectivity, and the (francophone) Quebec nation. These shifts are intentional; they are found in Bouchard's recent writings. He often provides ambiguous answers to the questions "What are we talking about when we talk about Quebec?" and "What are we referring to when we use the term *Quebec nation*?" In my opinion, this ambiguity, instead of reflecting a desire to convey the Quebec sociological experience in its irreducible complexity, reveals Bouchard's difficulty in finding a narrative form that successfully reconciles his scholarly and his political postulates. See, for example, the evasive argument he makes concerning the nation in Quebec and the Quebec collectivity in *Genèse des nations et cultures du nouveau monde. Essai d'histoire comparée* (Montreal: Boréal, 2000), 78ff.

17 Harshly criticizing the view of Quebec as a civic nation that is also several cultural or ethnic nations – the French-Canadian nation, anglophone nation, and Amerindian nations – Bouchard writes, "It seems [to me] that this conception should be rejected because it does not serve the interests of Quebec and its citizens well." "La réécriture de l'histoire nationale au Québec," 131 (translators' note: our translation).

18 *Dialogue sur les pays neufs*, chap. 11, "L'État."

19 G. Bouchard, "L'avenir de la nation comme 'paradigme' de la société québécoise," in *Les convergences culturelles dans les sociétés pluriethniques*, ed. Khadiyatoulah Fall et al. (Sillery: PUQ/CÉLAT, 1996), 159–68.

20 "La réécriture de l'histoire nationale au Québec," 121.

21 This assertion obviously only holds with respect to the overall representation of Quebec. For Bouchard, as for the vast majority of scholars, national history remains one area of historical research among many.

22 *La nation québécoise au futur et au passé*, 42–61.

23 See in particular *Quelques arpents d'Amérique. Population, économie, famille au Saguenay, 1838–1971* (Montreal: Boréal, 1996).

24 See, for example, G. Bouchard, *L'histoire comparée des sociétés neuves. Une autre perspective pour les études québécoises*, Grandes

conférences Desjardins (Montreal: McGill University, Québec Studies Program, 1999).

25 It must be admitted, however, that this is beginning to be less true, at least in academia. See, for example, Joseph-Yvon Thériault, *Critique de l'américanité. Mémoire et démocratie au Québec* (Montreal: Québec-Amérique, 2002); Jocelyn Maclure, *Quebec Identity: The Challenge of Pluralism* (Montreal/Kingston: McGill-Queen's University Press, 2003); Jacques Beauchemin, *L'histoire en trop. La mauvaise conscience des souverainistes québécois* (Montréal: VLB, 2002).

26 As is ultimately shown by his *Genèse des nations.*

27 G. Bouchard, *L'histoire comparée des collectivités neuves*; ibid., "Le Québec et le Canada comme collectivités neuves. Esquisse d'étude comparée," *Recherches sociographiques* 39, nos. 2–3 (1998): 219–48; ibid., *Entre l'Ancien et le Nouveau Monde. Le Québec comme population neuve et culture fondatrice* (Ottawa: Presses de l'Université d'Ottawa, 1996); *Genèse des nations*, chaps 1, 2, and 7.

28 It goes without saying that Bouchard uses the concepts of continuity and rupture as "ideal types" in the very Weberian sense. He points out, appropriately, that in practice the disengagement of the new collectivities from their metropolises has given rise to a large number of variants of the ideal processes. This being said, these variants, as is required for the pertinence of this model, are always related to the theoretical categories that give them meaning. Hence, the evolution of the new collectivities is seen ultimately from the perspective of continuity or rupture.

29 This, obviously, does not imply that he lacks critical perspective with respect to the historical development of the United States of America.

30 "Le Québec et le Canada comme collectivités neuves," 227 (translators' note: our translation). For a more detailed statement of this hypothesis, see *Genèse des nations*, 348–66.

31 "Le Québec et le Canada comme collectivités neuves," 227 (translators' note: our translation). See also *Genèse des nations,* chap. 4.

32 "Le Québec et le Canada comme collectivités neuves," 227 (translators' note: our translation); *Genèse des nations,* chap. 5 and p. 330–47.

33 *Genèse des nations*, 313–29.

34 G. Bouchard, "Une nation, deux cultures. Continuités et ruptures dans la pensée québécoise traditionnelle (1840–1960)," in *La construction d'une culture. Le Québec et l'Amérique française*, ed. G. Bouchard with Serge Courville (Sainte-Foy: PUL, 1993), 3–47; ibid., "L'ethnographie au secours de la nation. Mobilisation de la culture populaire par les lettrés canadiens-français (1850–1900)," in *Identité et cultures nationales. L'Amérique française en mutation*, ed. Simon Langlois (Sainte-Foy: PUL, 1995), 17–47; ibid., "Le Québec comme collectivité neuve. Le refus de l'américanité dans le discours de la survivance," in *Québécois et Américains. La culture québécoise aux XIX*[e] *et XX*[e] *siècles*, ed. G. Bouchard and Y. Lamonde (Montreal: Fides, 1995), 15–60.

35 This is the title of the long section in *Genèse des nations* analyzing the case of Quebec.

36 "Populations neuves, cultures fondatrices et conscience nationale en Amérique latine et au Québec," in *La nation dans tous ses états*, 45 (translators' note: our translation). In *Genèse des nations*, this same observation is repeated no less than three times in the same terms (60, 173, and 369).

37 "La réécriture de l'histoire nationale," 121.

38 G. Bouchard, *L'histoire comparée des collectivités neuves*, passim. For a convincing example of the effective use of comparativism in Bouchard's work, see his "Le Québec comme collectivité neuve. Le refus de l'américanité dans le discours de la survivance," 31 ff. The argument presented in chap. 2 of *Genèse des nations* is also quite defensible.

39 This expression is borrowed from Ronald Rudin, who has also criticized Bouchard's comparative approach. See his "Le rôle de l'histoire comparée dans l'historiographie québécoise," in *À propos de l'histoire nationale*, 103–13.

40 G. Bouchard, "Le Québec et le Canada comme collectivités neuves," 231 ff.

41 Ibid.

42 Ibid., 232.

43 People in the media, especially, have been seduced by Bouchard's arguments, and as a result he has gained considerable

influence in the public arena. Of course, the academic world has been more circumspect, as shown by the critiques published on his latest works.

44 See my article, "La production historienne courante portant sur le Québec et ses rapports avec la construction des figures identitaires d'une communauté communicationnelle," *Recherches sociographiques* 36, no. 1 (1995), 9–45."

45 G. Bouchard, *Quelques arpents d'Amérique*; ibid., "Marginality, Co-Integration and Change: Social History as a Critical Exercise," *Journal of the Canadian Historical Association*, New Series, vol. 8 (1997): 19–38.

46 On this topic, see the works of Yvan Lamonde.

47 To my mind, saying that Quebec's historical path was and is unique in no way implies that I am taking the perspective of exceptionalism.

48 G. Bouchard, *Entre l'Ancien et le Nouveau Monde. Le Québec comme population neuve et culture fondatrice* (Ottawa: PUO, 1995), 2. It should be noted that in *Genèse des nations* (182), he seems to retreat from this essentially pessimistic vision of Quebec history by opening up, as I myself advocate, to the ambivalence of Quebec identity and culture. In a conclusion that is surprising in view of his previous statements (and his previous works), Bouchard says that Quebec's culture is perhaps one of interstices, a culture that is seeking to define itself along oblique paths, drawing on all sources near and far, mixing and scattering all its heritages to create for itself a "bastard" place, a position as a sort of eccentric being, which allows it to express its disrespect toward the worlds that historically were its references (with which to define itself) and foils (against which to define itself).

49 See *La nation québécoise au futur et au passé*, 149n45, on Quebecers' difficulty in shedding a biological conception of collective origins, which would explain their reservations about considering Amerindians the "first Quebecers." See also the conclusion of *L'histoire comparée des collectivités neuves*, especially 54–5.

50 The argument he uses to justify his position, which verges on a counterfactual approach, is developed in his *L'histoire comparée des collectivités neuves*, p. 52–3. See also *Genèse des nations*, 49.

51 *Genèse des nations,* 49 (translators' note: our translation).
52 G. Bouchard, "Pour une nation québécoise. Contre le retour d'une pensée ethnique," in *Savoir et responsabilité,* ed. Michel de Sève and Simon Langlois (Quebec City: Nota Bene, 1999), 191–233; ibid., "Manifeste pour une coalition nationale."
53 This narrative structure is clearly evident in the article quoted: "Le Québec et le Canada comme collectivités neuves." It is repeated in a more didactic form in a small book written in collaboration with François and Guy Rocher, *Les Francophones québécois* (Montreal: Conseil scolaire de l'île de Montreal, 1991), especially chaps 3, 4, and 10. It is also implicit in his *Genèse des nations,* chap. 3.
54 This observation is also made by Ronald Rudin, who claims that in wanting to break with one representation of the past, the "revisionists" have gone much too far in the articulation of an alternative interpretation. Not surprisingly, this criticism was not well received by the "interested parties." See the debate published under the title "Y a-t-il une nouvelle histoire du Québec?" *Bulletin d'histoire politique* 4, no. 2 (1995): 3–74.
55 G. Bouchard, *Entre l'Ancien et le Nouveau Monde,* 9.
56 G. Bouchard, based on the work of John Hare, "Le Québec et le Canada comme collectivités neuves," 235.
57 G. Bouchard, *Entre l'Ancien et le Nouveau Monde,* 34.
58 It should be noted that for Bouchard the past has no inevitability. Clearly, what has happened must be seen as one possibility among many that could have occurred. It is therefore conceivable and appropriate, using the comparative method, to establish a list of possibilities and to envision the past other than as it was, and thus not to assume it is closed, but rather to pass judgment on the pattern of its fulfillment.
59 *La nation québécoise au futur et au passé,* 140.
60 F. Dumont, *Raisons communes* (Montreal: Boréal, 1995), chap. 3. It is well known how strongly Gérard Bouchard opposes Dumont's views on this issue, for which he has been harshly criticized by Serge Cantin, in "Nation et mémoire chez Fernand Dumont. Pour répondre à Gérard Bouchard," *Bulletin d'histoire politique* 9, no. 1 (fall 2000): 40–59. Bouchard's response was

scathing: "Sur le modèle de la nation québécoise et la conception de la nation chez Fernand Dumont," *Bulletin d'histoire politique* 9, no. 2 (winter 2001): 144–59. See also "Un 'bouchardisme' qui tient de la fabulation. Gérard Bouchard réplique à Serge Cantin," *Le Devoir*, 29 January 2001.

61 "La réécriture de l'histoire nationale au Québec," 140.

62 G. Bouchard, "Une francophonie nord-américaine," *La Presse*, 7 May 1998 (translators' note: our translation).

63 This equation was "formalized" by Yvan Lamonde – for didactic purposes only, as he has stated – as part of his work on the history of ideas in Quebec. The equation should be read as follows: to grasp Quebec's history and Quebecers' identity (Q), we need to subtract a little Frenchness (–F), add some Britishness (+GB), double the Americanness (USA^{2}), and reduce the Latinness (–R; *romanité* in French). See Lamonde, *Allégeances et dépendances. L'histoire d'une ambivalence identitaire* (Quebec City: Nota Bene, 2001).

64 *La nation québécoise au futur et au passé*, 11–14.

65 Ibid., 42–61.

66 Ibid., 92.

67 "Jeter les souches au feu de la Saint-Jean," *Le Devoir*, 24 March 1999. Wounded by the harsh response to this article by several critics, Bouchard felt it wise to more fully define his ideas. See his "Rectificatifs sur la nation, l'identité et la mémoire," *Le Devoir*, 5 May 1999.

68 Gérard Bouchard seems well aware of this when he says, with a certain hesitancy: "I think there exists in Quebec a collective space suitable for founding a cultural nation – and also a national culture or identity – that would be viable and legitimate, given the very great flexibility with which these concepts must be used. This space is fragile, of course, it is still largely in the process of being formed, but it exists." *La nation québécoise au futur et au passé*, 63 (translators' note: our translation).

69 For a nuanced view on this question, see Denys Delâge, "Autochtones, Canadiens, Québécois," in *Les espaces de l'identité*, ed. Laurier Turgeon, J. Létourneau, and Khadiyatoulah Fall (Sainte-Foy: Presses de l'Université Laval, 1998), 280–301.

70 See Jean-Jacques Simard, "La réduction des Amérindiens. Entre l'envers du Blanc et l'avenir pour soi," in *L'État et les minorités*, ed. Jean Lafontant (Saint-Boniface: Presses universitaires de Saint-Boniface / Éditions du Blé, 1998), 153–86.

71 See *Transferts culturels et métissages Amérique/Europe, XVIe-XXe siècle / Cultural Transfer, America and Europe: 500 years of interculturation*, ed. Laurier Turgeon, Denys Delâge, and Réal Ouellet (Quebec City: Presses de l'Université Laval, 1996).

72 D. Delâge, "Autochtones, Canadiens, Québécois."

73 G. Bouchard, *La nation québécoise au futur et au passé*, 149n45, rejects this objection out of hand, claiming that it is possible to establish such a line of descent between Native and non-Native peoples if we rid ourselves of a biological conception of collective origins. He cites the examples of the Mexicans and the Australians, who apparently have overcome this major problem of otherness, transforming yesterday's Other, completely foreign to the problems of the nation, into a perennial Self – as if such historical surgery, the ethics and esthetics of which are unsettling, could erase the effects of the past and give history a chance to begin again. In a subsequent article ("Rectificatifs sur la nation, l'identité et la mémoire," *Le Devoir*, 5 May 1999), Bouchard pulls back somewhat from this position, saying that his remarks were intended more to raise the problem of the workings of memory than to express a definitive opinion on the question of "our ancestors the Amerindians."

74 In the Bouchardian narrative, francophone Canadians living outside Quebec are "not in the picture." Not being part of the Quebec nation, they are not included in the history of Quebec.

75 I would like to say that I fully share Bouchard's desire to look at the period of the French regime without the customary image of the "Golden Age," and at the British regime without that of "Collective Downfall." See *La nation québécoise au futur et au passé*, 111 ff.

76 *Dialogue sur les pays neufs*, 188 ff.

77 See Serge Cantin, "J'impense, donc j'écris. Réponse à Jocelyn Létourneau," *Argument* 1, no. 2 (spring 1999): 139–42.

78 On this subjet, see Michel Seymour, "Plaidoyer pour la nation socio-politique," in *Nationalité, citoyenneté et solidarité*, 153–67.

79 For a more detailed discussion of these questions, see J. Létourneau, "Y a-t-il une nation québécoise? Est-il impératif qu'elle advienne? Une mise au point," *Argument* 5, no. 1 (fall 2002–winter 2003): 99–119.

80 It should be noted that the last ten lines are based on a very fine passage (67) in *La nation québécoise au futur et au passé.*

CHAPTER THREE

1 To appreciate and assess this text, the reader will have to accept the premise it is based on: that since Canada exists as an established country and the culmination of a historical experience, it necessarily poses the challenge of its narrativization. In other words, whatever one's conception of Canada, one cannot avoid the demand to write its history in the form of a narrative that traces its dynamics and provides a comprehensive synthesis. This said, the history can, of course, be shaped according to different narrative and interpretive frameworks in keeping with scholarly ethics. In this context, what history should be favoured? If one assumes, as I do, that the Canadian historical experience (within which the Quebec historical experience that was its starting point has a key place) is, despite the vicissitudes and wounds that have marked it, sufficiently positive to be pursued, one is immediately confronted with the delicate but unavoidable question of its possible future. Insofar as the future of collectivities is always in part predisposed by the horizons opened or closed by the interpreted past, it follows that the narrativization of what has been is an important, even crucial, element in the political enterprise of preparing the future of collectivities. Hence the interest of the question raised in this article: What history for the future of Canada?

2 I should nevertheless mention the efforts, which are more or less ideologically and politically oriented, of the Historica Foundation, the Dominion Institute, the Association for Canadian Studies, and similar organizations, as well as the series of major national conferences, the first three of which were held in Montreal, Winnipeg, and Halifax on topics directly related to the narrativization of the history of Canada.

3 These words are repeated in various documents from the Department of Canadian Heritage.

4 For a similar position, see the general introduction (4–5 in particular) of *As I Recall: Historical Perspectives,* ed. Institute for Research on Public Policy, with John Meisel, Guy Rocher, Arthur Silver (Montreal: IRPP, 1999).

5 H. Arendt, "Thinking and Moral Considerations," *Social Research* 38, no. 3 (fall 1971): 417–46.

6 See his "History and Rhetoric," trans. Thomas Epstein, in *The Social Responsibility of the Historian,* ed. Francois Bedarida (Providence, RI: Berghahn Books, 1994), 7–24, translation of "Histoire et rhétorique," *Diogène,* no. 168 (October–December 1994): 9–26. See also his *Time and Narrative,* trans. Kathleen McLaughlin and David Pellauer, 3 vols. (Chicago: University of Chicago Press, 1983–88), translation of *Temps et récit* (Paris: Seuil, 1985–88).

7 The use of the phrase "great national narrative" in no way implies that I envisage Canada as a nation. In fact, that question does not interest me here. Writing the history of the "Canadian nation" does not seem any more valid to me, academically or politically, than writing the history of the "Quebec nation" in Gérard Bouchard's sense, for example. To my mind, the expression "great national narrative" is merely another way of speaking of the great narrative overview of Canadian history.

8 This distress has taken three forms: criticism of the content of the narrative itself, complaining about Canadians' lack of historical knowledge, and denunciation of the control the American media, especially television, have over young people's memory.

9 See Michael Bliss, "Privatizing the Mind: The Sundering of Canadian History, the Sundering of Canada," *Journal of Canadian Studies,* 26, no. 4 (winter 1991–92): 5–17; Jack Granatstein, *Who Killed Canadian History?* (Toronto: Harper Collins, 1998), chap. 4. For a much more nuanced position, see Doug Owram, "Narrow Circles: The Historiography of Recent Canadian Historiography," *National History: A Canadian Journal of Enquiry and Opinion* 1, no. 1 (1997), 5–21.

10 Carl Berger, *The Writing of Canadian History: Aspects of English Canadian Historical Writing Since 1900* (Toronto: Oxford University Press, 1986), chap. 11; ibid., "Writings in Canadian History," in

Literary History of Canada: Canadian Literature in English, ed. W.H. New, 2d ed., vol. 4 (Toronto: University of Toronto Press, 1990), 293–332. It should be remembered that it was Ramsay Cook and J.M.S. Careless who, in some rather programmatic articles (Cook, "Canadian Centennial Celebrations," *International Journal,* 22, no. 4 (fall 1967): 663; Careless, "Limited Identities in Canada," *Canadian Historical Review* 50, no. 1 (1969): 1–10) both started and legitimized the pluralist shift in Canadian historiography.

11 This was especially evident in the case of the history of ethnic groups and cultural communities. See, on this subject, Roberto Perrin, "Writing about Ethnicity," in *Writing About Canada: A Handbook for Modern Canadian History,* ed. J. Schultz (Scarborough Ont.: Prentice-Hall, 1990), 201–30; ibid., "National Histories and Ethnic History in Canada," *Cahiers de recherche sociologique* 20 (1993): 113–28.

12 See the following for particularly sharp and valid criticisms of the positions taken by Granatstein in his previously cited book: Graham Carr, "Harsh Sentences: Appealing the Strange Verdict of *Who Killed Canadian History?" American Review of Canadian Studies* 28, nos. 1–2 (spring–summer 1998): 167–76; A.B. McKillop, "Who Killed Canadian History? A View from the Trenches," *Canadian Historical Review* 80, no. 2 (June 1999): 269–99.

13 For examples of unsatisfactory or limited responses, see the debate published under the title "Sundering Canadian History," *Journal of Canadian Studies* (summer 1992): 123–35; see also Veronica Strong-Boag, "Contested Space: The Politics of Canadian Memory," *Journal of the Canadian Historical Association* new series, 5 (1994): 3–17.

14 It should be noted that arguing in favour of national history in no way implies the disparagement of other kinds of history or of phenomena on the national territory that are not "national" in nature. The past, to repeat a truism, is infinitely complex and fine, and it can never be entirely or even mostly expressed in the narrative of the nation. In many respects, the concept of the nation is not necessarily even the most fruitful or the most subtle one for appreciating, embracing, and restoring the past of a collectivity. This being said, the challenge of writing an overview of

the history of Canada, insofar as this enterprise is legitimate and important (see note 1), is still on the agenda.

15 Jean-Marie Fecteau, "Between Scientific Enquiry and the Search for A Nation: Quebec Historiography as Seen by Ronald Rudin," *Canadian Historical Review* 80, no. 4 (December 1999): 641–66.

16 It should be understood that my remarks here are aimed at pluralistic overviews and not research. I have little criticism of the latter. It would never occur to me to discredit work because it lacks a metahistorical impact or is not of interest from the point of view of national history. To my mind, all research on all subjects is valid as long as it is carried out rigorously. It should further be noted that my criticism of pluralistic overviews does not concern the quality of the scholarly work, but rather the shortcomings of the narrative frameworks with respect to issues related to memory in a society in search of fruitful representations of itself.

17 Several writers who are otherwise positively disposed toward pluralistic history have pointed out that, while the old narrative paradigm of Canada has been deconstructed, no other "metavision" has been proposed to replace it. Indeed, its decline has not been total. While the perspective of "limited identities" now more or less prevails in all histories of Canada, the main parameters of the familiar history of Canada remain in place. Rather than occupying a central place, these parameters, including the "traditional" chronology that serves as their temporal support, are used as guideposts for the establishment of the new narrative, which often consists of thematic micro-narratives that do not conform to the single temporality of the gradual building of Canada. On this subject, see Gerald Friesen's contribution to the debate, entitled "New Wine or Just New Bottles? A Round Table on Recent Texts in Canadian History," *Journal of Canadian Studies* 30, no. 4 (winter 1995–96): 175–80.

18 There is a cliché common to all practitioners of pluralistic history: the idea of breaking away from the biases of the traditional narratives that gave a voice only to men, only to politicians, only to the military, only to central Canada, only to the majority, and only to the nation in the course of its fulfillment. This criticism is

not false. But is that a reason to abandon any claim to organizing the material of the past in the form a strong narrative of the Canadian historical experience?

19 We know how Lower, Creighton, and W.L. Morton, each in his own way, strived to create such narratives.

20 J.L. Granatstein, *Who Killed Canadian History?*

21 See Ramsay Cook, *Canada, Quebec and the Uses of Nationalism* (Toronto: McClelland and Stewart, 1986 [1966]). See also R. Bothwell, I. Drummond, and J. English, *Canada since 1945: Power, Politics and Provincialism* (Toronto: University of Toronto Press, 1981).

22 In his contribution to the book *Vive Quebec! New Thinking and New Approaches to the Quebec Nation* (ed. Michel Venne, trans. Robert Chodos and Louisa Blair [Toronto: Lorimer, 2001], translation of *Penser la nation québécoise* [Montreal: Québec-Amérique, 2000]), Charles Taylor says, quite rightly, that Quebecers of French-Canadian heritage must abandon their "essentialist myths" in order to envision the future of Quebec. The same reprimand could be made to (anglophone) Canadians about their own "essentialist myths," such as tolerance, the intrinsic superiority of the federal model, and consistent respect for individual rights. Canadian history clearly demonstrates the fragility of these three markers of identity.

23 We know that a large proportion of Canadians of Anglo-Celtic origin, commonly called English Canadians, long saw themselves as part of a kind of diaspora, which to a large extent explains their relationship to the mother country and their desire to see Canada closely tied to the Empire and then the Commonwealth. Following the British conquest, it should always be remembered, Canada developed as a colonial enterprise, in reaction against the American Revolution and the embryonic decolonization movement, which worried many loyalists.

24 It is wishful thinking to try to write a history of Canada that does not acknowledge the frequent, not to say continual, attempts by the English powers to assimilate, diminish, marginalize, and weaken francophones, particularly outside Quebec. Although the same was true for the Native peoples, they were not seen or

designated historically as a minority, but rather given the status of "wards of the Crown." The case of the Métis was "resolved" in a different way – by their repression as a group and the violent crushing of their desire to be distinctive within the Dominion of Canada.

25 This self-affirmation continues, especially by francophone Quebecers of French-Canadian heritage, who, concentrated in a territory constituted as a province, have been able to establish themselves in the Canadian landscape as a community that can neither be driven out nor assimilated. This was not a possibility for French Canadians living outside Quebec, in spite of all their resistance. That is why today the francophones dispersed through the country – with the exception of the Acadians in New Brunswick – do not, unlike Quebecers, constitute a major political force (or forces), only provincial lobbies with more or less influence, which rely on a certain tradition of biculturalism in the country, the federal official languages policy, and the rights of minorities in Canada. On this subject, see Joseph-Yvon Thériault, ed., *Francophonies minoritaires au Canada: l'état des lieux* (Moncton: Éditions d'Acadie, 1999).

26 See Kenneth McRoberts, *Misconceiving Canada: The Struggle for National Unity* (Toronto: Oxford University Press, 1997).

27 This statement obviously merits further development. In practice, the effect of the policy of multiculturalism (or that of interculturalism, in Quebec) is that diversity manages to be expressed in the social space of Canada, but without challenging the structuring power of the country's duality. By a folkloric view of diversity, I mean that it is difficult for a cultural group that does not have a critical mass of speakers in a circumscribed space to present anything more than a fetishized representation of itself in the theatre of public symbolism.

28 On this subject, see Daniel Francis, *National Dreams: Myth, Memory and Canadian History* (Vancouver: Arsenal Pulp Press, 1997), chap. 4.

29 It goes without saying that these power relationships have been and still are driven by powers and actors seeking space to spread out and grow, with the federal government, since 1867, necessarily

at the centre, itself an important place and structure of power. I should also point out that, in my view, it is by aligning themselves with the "Canadian" powers that have maintained and sustained them that "external" powers have been able in part to orient the country's development, especially since the mid-nineteenth century.

30 D. Owram, "Narrow Circles"; Roger Hall, "Whose History? Regarding Canada's History on Canada Day: The Consensus is that There Is No Consensus," *The Globe and Mail,* 28 June 1997.

31 For an example of this approach, see Margaret Conrad, Alvin Finkel, et al., *History of the Canadian Peoples,* 2 vols, 2d ed. (Toronto: Copp Clark, 1999); J.M. Bumsted, *The Peoples of Canada,* 2 vols (Toronto: Oxford University Press, 1992).

32 See Jean-Paul Bernard, "L'historiographie canadienne récente (1964–1994) et l'histoire des peuples du Canada," *Canadian Historical Review* 76, no. 3 (September 1995): 321–53.

33 Ibid.

34 It goes without saying that the francophones of Quebec constitute a minority in the context of Canada. The very high concentration of francophones within Quebec, however, makes francophone Quebecers a majority that, despite its constant demographic decline within Canada, has experienced not a loss, but a gain in its political importance, its force of cultural attraction, and its capacity to integrate and even assimilate people. In this sense, it is perfectly reasonable to see Quebecers as constituting a majority in Canada, a majority that, increasingly, encompasses all the inhabitants of the province. I will come back to this point in the last article in this book.

35 We can agree on the fact that religious affiliation can in certain cases slow or even modify any process of de-ethnicization and reacculturation.

36 With one major difference: while it is still the linguistic factor that makes possible the structural duality of Canada, the duality now tends to be quickly de-ethnicized and redefined in territorial terms, with Quebec on one side, Canada on the other.

37 Canada, Royal Commission on Aboriginal Peoples, *Report of the Royal Commission on Aboriginal Peoples,* vol. 1: *Looking Forward,*

Looking Back (Ottawa: Royal Commission on Aboriginal Peoples, 1996), 12ff.

38 Denys Delâge, "L'influence des Amérindiens sur les Canadiens et les Français au temps de la Nouvelle-France," *Lekton* 2, no. 2 (1992): 103–91; Olive Dickason, *First Nations: A History of Founding Peoples from Earliest Times* (Toronto: McClelland and Stewart, 1992).

39 Canada, *Report of the Royal Commission on Aboriginal Peoples*, 40–90; Bruce G. Trigger, "The Historian's Indian: Native Americans in Canadian Historical Writing from Charlevoix to the Present," *Canadian Historical Review* 67, no. 3 (1986): 315–42.

40 Denis Vaugeois, "Commentaires d'historien à partir du Rapport Erasmus-Dussault," *Recherches amérindiennes du Québec* 27, nos. 3–4 (1997): 123.

41 See Jean-Jacques Simard, "La réduction des Amérindiens. Entre l'Envers du Blanc et l'avenir pour soi," in *L'État et les minorités*, ed. Jean Lafontant (Saint-Boniface: Presses de l'Université de Saint-Boniface / Éditions du Blé, 1993), 153–86.

42 This comment is to some extent in keeping with the observations of Sylvie Vincent, "La version de l'Histoire présentée par la Commission royale permet-elle une meilleure compréhension entre Autochtones et non-Autochtones?" *Recherches amérindiennes du Québec* 27, nos. 3–4 (1997): 124–8.

43 For a similar position, see Louis-Edmond Hamelin, *Passer près d'une perdrix sans la voir, ou attitudes à l'égard des Autochtones*, Grande conférence Desjardins (Montreal: McGill University, Québec Studies Program, 1999). For a more idiosyncratic position, see Georges E. Sioui, *Pour une histoire amérindienne de l'Amérique* (Sainte-Foy: Presses de l'Université Laval, 1999 [1989]).

44 The question of whether this would be in a renewed federal structure or one of sovereignty-partnership does not interest me here.

45 In Canada, metropolitanism has always been connected to one or more relatively strong regionalist (and/or provincialist) structures while constantly being restrained in its hegemonic claims by those same structures.

46 See note 24.

47 But is it absolutely necessary to talk about "founding groups" or "founding peoples" to refer to the formal establishment of Canada as a state? Confederation took place in a specific economic and political context that enabled many actors to find an empirical solution to the apprehended impasses in their future development. At the time of Confederation, the united Canada was already structurally marked by linguistic-cultural dualism. The provisions of the BNA Act in no way countered this vital reality. Abandoning the notion of "founding peoples" absolutely does not imply a failure to recognize that Canada was formed and developed on the basis of duality.

48 The fact that the Amerindians call themselves the First Nations, for example, in no way implies that they subscribe to the Canadian identity. In truth, the Native peoples' Canadian identification is presumed or ascribed to them much more than it is a reality accepted or endorsed by those concerned.

49 Jean-Jacques Simard, "La réduction des Amérindiens." See also D. Delâge, "Autochtones, Canadiens, Québécois."

50 The creation of a new administrative and political territory in Canada – Nunavut – in which the vast majority of the population is Native (Inuit) and the agreement between the federal government and the Nisga'a in British Columbia are viewed positively by many observers.

51 See L. Turgeon, D. Delâge, and R. Ouellet, eds, *Transferts culturels et métissages, Amérique/Europe, XVIe-XXe siècle.*

52 It should be noted that this would be equivalent to writing a Native history of Canada whose objective was to show how the emergence of Canada as project, country, and state was perceived and experienced by the Native peoples. I agree that writing a Native history of the Native peoples is, or would be, a very different undertaking from those I have just described, if only because the Native peoples' conception of history is not the same as that of non-Natives, and because the non-Native factor and the Canada factor do not cover all of the Native peoples' past or all the complexity of that past. On this subject, see S. Vincent, "La version de l'Histoire présentée par la Commission royale." See

also Ken Coates, "Writing First Nations into Canadian History: A Review of Recent Scholarly Works," *Canadian Historical Review* 81, no. 1 (March 2000): 99–114.

53 S. Vincent, "La version de l'Histoire présentée par la Commission royale."

54 To borrow the title of a history textbook published at the time of the centennial of Confederation: P.G. Cornell, J. Hamelin, F. Ouellet, and M. Trudel, *Canada: Unity in Diversity* (Toronto: Holt, Rinehart and Winston, 1967). It is interesting to note the shift that took place in the title of the French translation of the book: *Canada: unité et diversité* (Montreal: Holt, Rinehart and Winston, 1968). I would like to thank Christian Laville for drawing my attention to this detail.

CHAPTER FOUR

1 Among his best-known films are *Traître ou patriote (Traitor or Patriot)* (2000), *Le Mouton noir (The Black Sheep)* (1992), *Alias Will James* (1988), *Comme en Californie* (1983), *Ixe 13* (1971); his books include *Une histoire américaine* (1986), *Les Têtes à Papineau* (1981), *L'Isle au dragon* (1976) (*Dragon Island* [1978]), *D'amour, P.Q.* (1972), *Salut Galarneau!* (1967) (*Hail Galarneau!* [1970]).

2 French original: *Le Sort de l'Amérique* (Montreal: National Film Board of Canada, 1996). Quotations are from the English version (1997), subtitles by Robert Gray.

3 Jacques Godbout, *Le Sort de l'Amérique*, screenplay, (Paris/Montreal: K-Films/Boréal, 1997), back cover (translators' note: our translation).

4 Born in 1968, Philippe Falardeau was a prize-winner on a popular television show on Radio-Canada, *La course autour du monde*. He worked on the research and script for Godbout's documentary.

5 Playwright, man of letters, and polemicist, René-Daniel Dubois has in recent years devoted a great deal of energy to political debate on the place of art and culture in society. With Godbout and Falardeau, he was a scriptwriter for *The Fate of America* in addition to contributing to the research.

6 The idea of the Langoliers as devourers of identity and presence came to me after I watched a televised miniseries based on a fantasy novella by Stephen King.

7 In the film, Laurier Lapierre, a historian and communicator as well as a senator, presents an iconoclastic version of the Battle of the Plains of Abraham. In his view, the event marked the defeat of the French by the English; it did not represent a defeat for the Canadiens, who must absolutely be distinguished from the French in the subsequent history of Canada. For further details on Lapierre's position, see his book *1759: The Battle for Canada* (Toronto: McClelland and Stewart, 1990). It should be noted that in the French translation, the title of the book is slightly different, suggesting the possibility of another meaning (*1759: la bataille du Canada* (Montreal: Le Jour, 1992).

8 It should be said that his words are far from clear and that his impressionistic formulation may be understood in many ways. Personally – and without implying that this is Godbout's view – I do not endorse the idea that it is possible to articulate a useful history as one can tell a useful lie, for a higher political purpose. In my view, no lying history could serve as the basis for political (re)conciliation or give rise to lasting happiness. The challenge for the interpreter is rather, from a rigorous intellectual position, to discover the narrative thread that prevents forgetting while making it possible to go beyond the wounds, the unifying thread that forbids forgiveness while making it inescapable.

9 Paul Ricœur, *Time and Narrative*, trans. Kathleen McLaughlin and David Pellauer, 3 vols. (Chicago: University of Chicago Press, 1984–88), translation of *Temps et récit* (Paris: Le Seuil, 1983–88).

CHAPTER FIVE

1 Serge Cantin, *Ce pays comme un enfant. Essais sur le Québec (1988–1996)* (Montreal: L'Hexagone, 1997).

2 I am using the term Québécois to refer exclusively to francophones who live in the province of Quebec and know or recognize the canons of history and memory by which this historically constituted community remembers itself, speaks itself, and repre-

sents itself to others. I also speak of them, as in the title of this article, as Quebecers of French-Canadian heritage.

3 A commentator on the work of Fernand Dumont, Serge Cantin has publicly presented himself in recent years as one of those who persist in seeing the condition of the Québécois (of French-Canadian heritage) as one of alienation, external oppression, and *la survivance*. For example, see his "Emerging from Survival Mode," in *Vive Quebec! New Thinking and New Approaches to the Quebec Nation,* ed. Michel Venne, trans. Robert Chodos and Louisa Blair (Toronto: Lorimer, 2001), 49–58.

4 Translators' note: our translation.

5 For more evidence of this, see the previously cited works by Serge Gagnon as well as R. Rudin, *Making History in Twentieth-Century Quebec* (Toronto: University of Toronto Press, 1997).

6 To borrow a particularly strong and moving formulation of Cantin's. Saint-Sauveur is a parish in the lower town of Quebec City, whose residents are largely poor. "Viarge" (the Holy Virgin in patois) is a common swear-word used by Cantin to evoke the wretched condition of Saint-Sauveur, and by extension French Quebec.

7 See R. Rudin, "Revisionism and the Search for a Normal Society"; J. Létourneau, "L'historiographie comme miroir, écho et récit de Nous Autres"; ibid., "The Current Great Narrative of Quebecois Identity," *The South Atlantic Quarterly* 94, no. 4 (fall 1995): 1039–54.

8 "L'avenir de la nation comme 'paradigme' de la société québécoise," in *Les convergences culturelles dans les sociétés pluriethniques,* ed. Khadiyatoulah Fall et al. (Sillery: PUQ/CÉLAT, 1996), 166 (translators' note: our translation).

9 "Des universitaires sur la planète Hollywood," *Le Devoir,* 12 August 1998 (translators' note: our translation). In his article, Cornellier – a teacher at the Cégep de Joliette who has a weekly column on Quebec non-fiction in *Le Devoir* – castigated the naivety of a group of intellectuals who, supported by a poll, recognized the Americanness of the Québécois, which to him was a sign of irresponsible complacency on the part of those (the intellectuals) whose duty is to stand up against neo-colonial alienation. The

relationship of the Québécois to Americanness has in recent years become one of the most hotly debated questions in Quebec. On this subject, see Joseph-Yvon Thériault, *Critique de l'américanité. Mémoire et démocratie au Québec* (Montreal: Québec-Amérique, 2000). See also G. Bouchard, responding to his critics, "L'américanité: un débat mal engagé," *Argument* 4, no. 2 (spring–summer 2002): 159–79.

10 Quoted in F. Dumont, *La Vigile du Québec. Octobre 1970: l'impasse?* (Montreal: Hurtubise HMH, 1971), 10 (translators' note: our translation).

11 Translators' note: our translation. Poet and *chansonnier* Félix Leclerc, in the final years of his life and for some time after his death in 1988 – he is little remembered by young people today – personified the Québécois rebelling against the conditions of his alienation and seeking, through the rediscovery of the sources of *québécitude* (he lived on Île d'Orléans, the symbolic origin of the French nation in America), to regain the essence of an unalienated identity. See Geneviève Leblanc, "Félix Leclerc en tant que figure rassembleuse d'une communauté mémorielle. Incursion au cœur de l'identitaire québécois" (master's thesis, Université Laval, 1998).

12 One senses the presence of the Christian cosmogony.

13 I mean by *country* the culture that exists and is expressed in a real or virtual place. To love one's country means being accountable to the culture, and therefore the group, that exists in a geographic or symbolic space of reciprocity.

14 On the importance of Dumont in the intellectual landscape of Quebec, see my comments above (chap. 1, note 11).

15 By *intellectuals*, I am referring to all those people who, by virtue of their positions or vocations, produce, fuel, shape, and echo the public discourse. By *major* intellectuals, I mean those who have built the national system of references and are recognized as such in the common consciousness.

16 On this point, see the literature cited in note 7.

17 For a similar argument, see Diane Lamoureux, "Le peuple problématique," in *Repères en mutation. Identité et citoyenneté dans le Québec contemporain*, ed. Jocelyn Maclure and Alain G. Gagnon

(Montreal: Québec-Amérique, 2001), 181–203. See also J. Létourneau, "Y a-t-il une nation québécoise? Est-il impératif qu'elle advienne? Une mise au point," *Argument* 5, no. 1 (fall 2002–winter 2003): 99–119.

18 Using the concept of a full-fledged society means giving oneself as an observer the means to see how a society becomes integrated through a complete representation of itself. It also means, inevitably, providing an overall definition of the society that contributes to the process of constructing a complete representation. Between the society in constant tension with itself and its complete representation, a positive or negative relationship is established that is constantly being shaped by actors demanding, supplying, and expecting new references. This is how representations of the full-fledged society follow one another as societies evolve in rhythms that are sometimes convergent, sometimes divergent.

The anecdotal history of the concept of the full-fledged society in Quebec has been summarized by Gilles Bourque, Jules Duchastel, and André Kuzminski as follows: "Introduced in the 1950s in discussions on the pertinence of the concept of folk society for understanding francophone Quebec, the concept of a full-fledged society made it possible in the 1960s to move from the idea of 'French-Canadian society' to that of 'Québécois society.' It was no longer a matter of thinking about the French-Canadian ethnic group within Canada as a 'society,' but of producing the representation of Quebec as a full-fledged society and most often as a potential nation-state." (From "Les grandeurs et les misères de la société globale au Québec," *Cahiers de recherche sociologique* 28 [1997]: 8 [translators' note: our translation].)

19 On this concept, see pages 67 to 69 above. See also J. Létourneau, "Passer à l'avenir. Réactualiser la canadianité," in *Canadian Distinctiveness in the XXIst Century / La distinction canadienne au XXIe siècle*, ed. Chad Gaffield and Karen Gould (Ottawa: University of Ottawa Press, 2003), 29–45.

20 *Genèse de la société québécoise* (Montréal: Boréal, 1993), 335–6.

21 "If I lived in France or Great Britain, I would not be a nationalist, but here I am one by necessity, given the fragility of my society

in North America. I reject the claim that one cannot be both nationalist and humanist." (Translators' note: our translation.) This quotation is taken from Pierre Cayouette, "Fernand Dumont, un phare pour la société québécoise," *Le Devoir,* 3–4 May 1997.

22 Without overemphasizing Dumont's conception of the nation, let me say that he saw it in a somewhat utopian way as a human and political community, rather than as a legal entity strictly bound or beholden to the structure of the state. The "nationalist vigilance" he called on intellectuals, in particular, to exercise was intended to protect the former. The fate of the latter was apparently of less concern to him, especially when its future was linked to base partisan interests. It must be acknowledged that this position and this distinction, while admirable in theory, are less clear in practice. On these questions, see his *Raisons communes* (Montreal: Boréal, 1997), chap. 3.

23 On these questions, see Fernand Dumont, *L'avenir de la mémoire* (Quebec City: Nuit Blanche, 1995).

24 It should be understood that to say he is reflecting *from a place* and not *on a subject* in no way implies the absence of a critical stance in Dumont, or the subordination of his "nationalist vigilance" to base partisan interests. The fact remains, however, that it is a delicate position. On this subject, see F. Dumont, *Raisons communes,* chaps 10 and 11.

25 I am speaking of transcendence here in the sense of going beyond, advancing, rising, with no teleological, theological, or mystical connotations.

26 "Ce pays comme un enfant," in Serge Cantin, *Ce pays comme un enfant* (Montreal: L'Hexagone, 1997), 15 (translators' note: our translation).

27 But nevertheless in light of the atmosphere permeating Cantin's arguments throughout the book.

28 This is the original meaning of the word *infant*. We also know how prominent the idea of "misery of being" ["misère à être"] and "difficulty [misère] of speaking and expressing oneself" are in Dumont for describing the identity of francophone Quebecers, whom he sees as marked by an alienated and alienating silence that testifies to their being rejected or marginalized in history.

29 I am using *intellectual* in the sense of someone whose role is to speak or to tell, just as others are responsible for doing.

30 This idea that French Quebec has not yet reached adulthood, for reasons related to the assimilation of a negative self-consciousness, was actually put forward by Dumont. I quote: "But were not the long period of colonialism we endured, our longing and jealousy regarding France and the United States, our false self-consciousness, a pathetic way of being in the world? A people that refuses to be adult out of contempt for itself is a poor partner." Fernand Dumont, *Raisons communes,* 75 (translators' note: our translation).

31 Fernand Dumont, "Le père et l'héritage," *Interprétation* 3, nos. 1–2 (January–June 1969): 11–23. On the idea of symbolic paternity in the Québécois imaginary, see François Ouellet, "Passer au rang du Père pour passer à l'avenir," *Argument* 4, no. 2 (2002): 40–56.

32 Jean Royer, "Le poète de la 'part de l'ombre,'" *Le Devoir,* 10–11 May 1997.

33 Fernand Dumont, "Peuple sans parole," *Liberté* 7, no. 5 (September–October 1965): 405 (translators' note: our translation).

34 Ibid., *Raisons communes,* 245 (translators' note: our translation).

35 Ibid., chap. 10.

36 Dumont, *L'avenir de la mémoire,* 17–18 (translators' note: our translation).

37 Fernand Dumont, *Récit d'une immigration* (Montreal: Boréal, 1997), 172 (translators' note: our translation).

38 *Ce pays comme un enfant,* 189 (translators' note: our translation).

CHAPTER SIX

1 J. Létourneau, "La production historienne courante portant sur le Québec et ses rapports avec la construction des figures identitaires d'une communauté communicationnelle," *Recherches sociographiques* 36, no. 1 (1995): 9–45.

2 This reproblematization of the Quebec historical experience is described (and criticized) by Ronald Rudin in his well-known article "Revisionism and the Search for a Normal Society:

A Critique of Recent Quebec Historical Writing," *Canadian Historical Review* 68, no. 1 (1992): 30–61.

3 For a detailed view of economic and social development in the different regions of Quebec, see the series of books published by the IQRC and, subsequently, the INRS – Société et culture in the collection "Régions du Québec."

4 On this subject, see Lucia Ferretti, *Brève histoire de l'Église catholique au Québec* (Montreal: Boréal, 1999).

5 This diagnosis is even endorsed by some prominent sovereignists. See Jean-François Lisée, "Les dix mythes de l'économie québécoise," *L'Action nationale* 92, no. 2 (February 2002): 47–76.

6 J. Létourneau, "Put the Future Behind Us," *The Globe and Mail*, 25 June 2001, p. A11.

7 While not going so far in his own views, through his empirical studies Yvan Lamonde has provided a lot of material for this thesis. See two of his most recent books: *Allégeances et dépendances. L'histoire d'une ambivalence identitaire* (Quebec City: Nota Bene, 2001) and *Histoire sociale des idées au Québec (1760–1896)* (Montreal: Fides, 2000).

8 Hockey player Maurice Richard, to whom Quebecers paid extraordinary tribute when he died, was the archetypal figure of the rebel. Pierre Trudeau, too, who was also admired in Quebec for certain of his personality traits, embodied the figure of the dissident or non-conformist. See J. Létourneau, "Pierre-Elliott Trudeau, le Québec et les Québécois," *Le Devoir*, 4 October 2000; "Trudeau fought to break bonds of Duplessis society," *The National Post*, 2 October 2000.

9 This view equating francophone Quebecers' "wait-and-see approach" with misery and *la survivance* is tirelessly repeated by Quebec thinkers and essayists, including Jean Larose, Pierre Vadeboncœur, Serge Cantin, and even Fernand Dumont. It seems that the generation of intellectuals that is now, quietly, asserting itself in the public space in Quebec is seeking to break with this equation. On this subject, see Stéphane Kelly, ed., *Les idées mènent le Québec. Essais sur une sensibilité historique* (Quebec City: Presses de l'Université Laval, 2003).

10 To me, the concept of generation does not refer primarily to age – although age is not insignificant – but to the situation of the actors in relation to the events and representations associated with the Quiet Revolution. On this basis, we can distinguish between the fathers of that revolution and the(ir) heirs, driven by an imaginary and an identity that, while they overlap, are nevertheless not mutually reducible. See Stéphane Kelly, ed., *Les idées mènent le Québec,* Introduction.

11 I would like to remind readers that I am focusing here exclusively on Quebecers of French-Canadian heritage, a community whose history must be distinguished from that of Canadian francophones although it is obviously related.

12 On this subject, see F. Dumont, *Genèse de la société québécoise* (Montréal: Boréal, 1993).

13 For a nuanced position on the political situation in Lower Canada in the 1830s, see Allan Greer, "Rebellion Reconsidered," *Canadian Historical Review* 76, no. 1 (1995): 1–18; Yvan Lamonde, "L'ambivalence historique du Québec à l'égard de sa continentalité: circonstances, raisons et signification," in *Québécois et Américains. La culture québécoise aux XIXe et XXe siècles,* ed. G. Bouchard and Y. Lamonde (Montreal: Fides, 1995), 61–84.

14 For the period 1867 to 1917, see Gilles Gougeon's interview with Réal Bélanger published in G. Gougeon, *Histoire du nationalisme québécois. Entrevues avec sept spécialistes* (Montreal: VLB-SRC, 1993), 51–86.

15 J.-Y. Thériault, ed., *Francophonies minoritaires au Canada* (Moncton: Éditions d'Acadie, 1999).

16 Pierre E. Trudeau, "Some Obstacles to Democracy in Quebec," *Canadian Journal of Economics and Political Science* 24, no. 3 (August 1958): 297–311, and "La province de Québec au moment de la grève," in *La grève de l'amiante,* ed. P.E. Trudeau (Montreal: Éditions du Jour, 1970 [1956]), 3–91.

17 For Trudeau, reforming federalism did not mean accommodating the ambivalence of (francophone) Quebecers. On the contrary, it meant increasingly promoting, even, if necessary, forcing, their positive and equitable integration into Canada. It

was this logic of forced salvation by Canada, the Quebecers' country, that propelled Chrétien and Dion's crusade at the beginning of this century against Quebecers' tendency to take refuge in their intertwined ties. On this subject, see Stéphane Dion, *Straight Talk: on Canadian Unity* (Montreal/Kingston: McGill-Queen's University Press, 1999).

18 For more details on this view of things, see J. Létourneau, "La Révolution tranquille, catégorie identitaire du Québec contemporain," in *Duplessis. Entre la Grande noirceur et la société libérale,* ed. Alain G. Gagnon and Michel Sarra-Bournet (Montreal: Québec-Amérique, 1997), 95–118.

19 René Lévesque, *Option Québec* (Montreal: Editions de l'Homme, 1968).

20 On this subject, see the series of articles published in *The Gazette* from 29 May to 6 June 1999, under the general title "The New Anglos." See also Martha Radice, *Feeling Comfortable? The Urban Experience of Anglo Montrealers* (Quebec City: Presses de l'Université Laval, 2000).

21 See Gary Caldwell, *La culture publique commune: les règles du jeu politique au Québec et les fondements de ces règles* (Quebec City: Nota Bene, 2001).

22 Sherry Simon, "Crossing Town: Montreal in Translation," *Maisonneuve* 3 (Spring 2003): 16–21.

23 Richard Nadeau and Jean-Marc Léger, "L'appui à la souveraineté croît avec l'inquiétude linguistique," *Le Devoir,* 27 April 2000.

24 This is the title of a book by this controversial essayist whose views on English Canada are, to say the least, as simplistic and ignorant as those of Diane Francis on Quebec.

25 J. Létourneau, "La nouvelle figure identitaire du Québécois. Essai sur la dimension symbolique d'un consensus social en voie d'émergence," *British Journal of Canadian Studies* 6, no. 1 (1991): 17–38.

26 For some tidbits of history on this expression, which was not invented by Lesage, see Dale C. Thomson, *Jean Lesage and the Quiet Revolution* (Toronto: Macmillan, 1984).

27 For an even richer understanding of Jean Lesage's thought and the Quebec Liberal Party's constitutional position, see Dale C.

Thomson, *Jean Lesage*; Vincent Lemieux, *Histoire du Parti libéral du Québec* (Sainte-Foy: Presses de l'Université Laval, 1997); Claude Morin, *Mes premiers ministres* (Montreal: Boréal, 1991).

28 In the wake of the failure of the Meech Lake Accord, some members of the Quebec Liberal Party, disappointed by the turn of events and wanting to restart political and constitutional debate on the basis of a statement of Quebec's demands, published a report – commonly referred to by the name of its author, Jean Allaire – that elicited a good deal of reaction in Quebec. This report included a list of powers and areas of jurisdiction that would have to be returned to Quebec as part of a process of renewal of federalism.

29 A mandarin in the Quebec civil service in the 1960s, Jacques Parizeau, a brilliant man but one with set ideas and, it must be admitted, a gift for polarizing feelings in his private and public life, was premier of Quebec from 1994 to 1995. Associated with the hardliners in the sovereignist movement, of which he saw himself as one of the leading figures, he set in motion the referendum process of 1995. Since his resignation, in 1995, as premier of Quebec and leader of the Parti Québécois, he has tried to gain support for his views on the political and constitutional future of Quebec through often ill-timed declarations. Despite his charisma and the fact that he is one of the best orators Quebec has produced, his views are gradually being marginalized in the public arena.

30 In practice, it seems that the constitutive social relationships of Quebec society have, at least for the time being, given rise "only" to a collectivity that wants prosaic happiness.

31 It is in the context of this strategy that the passage of the Clarity Act by the federal government at the instigation of Chrétien and Dion must be understood.

32 The scandal, first revealed in spring 2002, over the funding of federal advertising in Quebec reveals the full extent of the Chrétien government's strategy in this area.

33 For an example of this type of argument, see Max Nemni, "Le mythe du fédéralisme renouvelé est mort," *Le Devoir*, 18 October 1999.

34 For example: Reed Scowen, *Time to Say Goodbye* (Toronto: McClelland and Stewart, 1999); David J. Bercuson and Barry Cooper, *Deconfederation: Canada without Quebec* (Toronto: Key Porter, 1991); Jacques Parizeau, *Pour un Québec souverain* (Montreal: VLB, 1997). The list could go on.

Index